Embodied Protests

INTERPRETATIONS OF CULTURE IN THE NEW MILLENNIUM

Norman E. Whitten Jr., General Editor

A list of books in the series appears at the end of the book.

Embodied Protests

Emotions and Women's Health in Bolivia

MARIA TAPIAS

UNIVERSITY OF ILLINOIS PRESS
Urbana, Chicago, and Springfield

© 2015 by the Board of Trustees
of the University of Illinois
All rights reserved
Manufactured in the United States of America
1 2 3 4 5 C P 5 4 3 2 1
∞ This book is printed on acid-free paper.

Library of Congress Cataloging-in-Publication Data
Tapias, Maria, author.
Embodied protests: emotions and women's health in Bolivia / Maria Tapias.
p. cm. — (Interpretations of culture in the new millennium)
ISBN 978-0-252-03917-1 (cloth : alk. paper)
ISBN 978-0-252-08074-6 (pbk. : alk. paper)
ISBN 978-0-252-09715-7 (ebook)
I. Title.
II. Series: Interpretations of culture in the new millennium.
[DNLM: 1. Psychophysiologic Disorders—etiology—Bolivia. 2. Socioeconomic Factors—Bolivia. 3. Culture—Bolivia. 4. Emotions—Bolivia. 5. Women—psychology—Bolivia. WM 90]
HQ1537
305.40984—dc23   2014035712

For Xavi

Contents

Acknowledgments   ix

Introduction: Embodied Protests, Emotions, and Failing Socialities   1

1. Neoliberalism on the Ground: Political, Economic, and Social Landscapes   25
2. Physicality's Sociality and Sociality's Physicality: Fluid Boundaries of the Body   43
3. The Intergenerational Embodiment of Social Suffering   56
4. Anxious Ambitions and the Financing of Tranquility   76
5. Moving Sentiments: Emotions and Migration   105

Conclusion   127

Notes   133
Glossary   137
References   141
Index   155

Acknowledgments

The personal and intellectual debts accrued during the writing of a book are extensive and a humbling reminder of the generosity and kindness of many people and institutions who have enabled, supported, nurtured, and encouraged my research for more than two decades. I am, first and foremost, deeply grateful to the women of Punata—*comadres*, friends, and caretakers who welcomed me into their homes, shared food and drink with me, and who patiently shared their sorrows, fears, hopes, and aspirations with me. Although I cannot name each of them and have used pseudonyms throughout this book, their reflections helped me view the body, health, and emotions in new ways. Without their deep engagement and trust, this book would not have been possible. Any omissions or unintended misrepresentations within these pages are, of course, my own fault.

Several grants, fellowships, and awards have supported my fieldwork, research, and writing. Preliminary field trips were funded by an ethnographic training grant supported by the National Science Foundation and the Center for Latin American and Caribbean Studies at the University of Illinois, Urbana-Champaign. The extended fieldwork was generously funded by the Joint Committee on Latin American Studies of the Social Science Research Council and by a U.S. Student Fulbright Grant. Generous funding from the University of Illinois, Urbana-Champaign and Grinnell College made it possible for me to write and undertake several return trips to Bolivia as well as begin fieldwork in Spain with Bolivian migrants. I am very grateful to all these institutions for their support.

This project has been mentored and intellectually shaped by many people who merit special recognition. I am particularly indebted to Norman

Whitten, whose continued support and encouragement through the many ups and downs of the writing process were invaluable. It is a privilege to count on the support of a mentor well beyond one's graduate school years. I extend special thanks to Bill Kelleher, whose kindness, insights, and gentle guidance is terribly missed by many of his students. I am also deeply grateful for the insights and feedback from Nancy Abelman, Clark Cunningham, Alma Gottlieb, Alejandro Lugo, Janet Keller, Andy Orta, and Clodoaldo Soto. I am very proud to call each of them an important part of my intellectual genealogy. My work also greatly benefited from countless discussions with colleagues and the support of friends in Bolivia, the United States, and across the globe: Lisa Avalos, Sandra Hamid, Gina Hunter, and Jill Leonard deserve heartfelt thanks along with Debbie Boehm, Charles Briggs, Clara Mantini Briggs, Pamela Calla, Victor Hugo Callisaya, John Fennell, Richard Freeman, Brigittine French, Michael Goldman, Nelly Gonzalez, John Hammond, David Hopping, Ronnie Kann, Tom Kruse, Heather Lobban-Viravong, Aurolyn Luykx, Ladona Martin-Frost, Enrique Mayer, Johanna Meehan, Claire Moisan, Susan Paulson, Sarah Phillips, Judith Pintar, Nancy Postero, Maria Ester Pozo, Liz Queathem, Denise Roth, Gemma Sala, Ralph Savarese, Miriam Shakow, Mark Schneider, Rachel Schurman, Simone Sidwell, Suzanne Simon, Maura Strassberg, Arlene Torres, Gaku Tsuda, Krista Van Vleet, Katie Wiegele, Jill Wightman, and Jonathan Zilberg. I am also grateful to my colleagues in the Department of Anthropology at Grinnell College for their support and collegiality. Special thanks to Sondi Burnell, Caroline Bailey, Heather Riggs, and Gabielle Robinson-Bajuscik for their research assistance, transcriptions, and runs to the library, and to Juana Rojas and Silvia Jaldin for help in the field. The staff at the University of Illinois press patiently helped bring this project to its completion, and a special thanks is extended to Danny Nasset, Julie Gay, and John Bealle for indexing.

I wish to thank my mother and father, Marina and Oscar, who have been endless sources of encouragement and support. My father passed away before this book was completed, but his love of learning, his intellectual curiosity, and his empathy for the human condition have always been and will continue to be sources of inspiration. My mother has modeled for me what it means to be mindful of what it might be like to walk in the shoes of others and taught me to be true to my dreams. My parents-in-law Maria Antonia Tur and Antonio Escandell welcomed me into their hearts and home since the first time I visited them in Spain and have always been a source of wisdom and laughter for me. I also wish to thank my brothers, Carlos, Oscar, and Tony, who in their own quiet "Tapias" way have always cheered me on.

Thanks also to my sister-in-law, Eva, my niece Christine and my nephews Paul and Xavi, as well as all my extended family in New York and in Bolivia, most particularly my tia Norah and Uncle Tony, my tia Teresa and tio Mario, tio Rafy and tia Quely, tio Jaime, tia Teresa, tio Enrique as well as my numerous "primos hermanos." Although I have now spent most of my adult life in the Midwest, what makes it "home" are wonderful friends and a community of people who must also be thanked: Cheri and Gary Cederlund, Michelle Devlin, Valentina and Artun Doumanian, Tony Gabriele and Elana Joram, Mark and Mary Grey, Deedee Heisted and Jeff Funderburk, Farah and Ali Kashef, Konrad Sadkowski and Alicja Boruta-Sadkowski, Francesca Soans and Gereon Kopf, Isabela Varela and Greg Bruess as well as the rest of the Cedar Falls/Waterloo crew.

Finally, my deepest thanks go to my husband, partner in life, intellectual sounding board, and friend, Xavier Escandell, and our two sparkling and magical daughters, Marina and Gemma, who ground us amid the chaos of our household. Xavi has been the tireless and best possible supporter, advocate, and partner for all things work and life related. He has read countless drafts of my work, and his keen insights have helped push me to further refine the arguments made in this book. Those who know him know he is, indeed, larger than life—and, for all those who have asked: Yes, I have laughed nearly every day since 1999 when we first met. This book is lovingly dedicated to him.

Author's Note

The introduction and chapter 3 contain material that has previously appeared in "Emotions and the Intergenerational Embodiment of Social Suffering in Rural Bolivia," *Medical Anthropology Quarterly* 20, no. 3 (2006): 399–415, and in "Always Ready and Always Clean? Competing Discourses of Breastfeeding, Infant Illness and the Politics of Mother-blame in Bolivia," *Body and Society* 12, no. 2 (2006): 83–108. Portions of chapter 5 appeared in "Transnational Lives, Travelling Emotions and Idioms of Distress among Bolivian Migrants in Spain," *Journal of Ethnic and Migration Studies* 36, no. 3: 407–23, and in "Not in the Eyes of the Beholder: Envy among Bolivian Migrants in Spain," *International Migration* 49, no. 6 (2011): 74–94. These selections are used with permission and appreciation. The map used in the book was graciously developed by Kathryn Kamp, despite the numerous demands on her time. The beautiful painting on the cover is by Antonio Mariaca and is titled "Procesión en rojo"; it is used with permission. All photographs and translations were undertaken by the author.

Introduction
Embodied Protests, Emotions, and Failing Socialities

On a winter morning in 1998, before the first rays of the bright Andean sun were able to catch Teresa in bed, she carefully bundled her weakened granddaughter Carmen in several warm layers, nestling her between the folds of an *awayo*, a colorful carrying cloth. Teresa, a fifty-four-year-old Quechua grandmother, gathered the opposite corners of the awayo and in one fell swoop, with the expertise and confidence of someone who had carried many an infant this way, gently swung the child onto her back, securing the cloth's corners into a firm double knot across her chest. At the request of Carmen's parents, who had emigrated to Argentina in search of employment ten months earlier, Teresa then made her way to the local hospital, where she hoped her granddaughter's severe case of diarrhea would be treated. They arrived at the nurse's station at the crack of dawn, took a number, and awaited care for several hours.

As the emergency room slowly filled with patients, several mothers and grandmothers asked Teresa what was wrong with the child. Teresa explained that the day before, while playing, Carmen had been frightened by an army airplane that flew over their house's patio. Just over the mountain range north of Punata, where Teresa and her grandchild lived, is the Chapare, a coca-growing region. Throughout the 1990s the U.S. military and the Drug Enforcement Agency's (DEA) presence were heavily felt in the region as prominent actors supporting the global "war on drugs." Occasionally, such jets could be seen flying low over this range, sometimes creating a sonic boom that could jolt you out of your seat in the relative tranquility of town. The women all concurred that the child had a strong case of *susto*, and as such it was best for Teresa to secure the care of a healer. Susto, a folk illness found throughout Latin America, develops after a profound fright that causes a person's soul, or *ánimo*, to leave the body. It was obvious to the mothers (and to Teresa) that the illness affecting the child was not to be addressed by a doctor. Carmen's parents, however, no longer believed in such ailments and had pleaded from afar for Teresa to take the child to the doctor.

The women in the emergency room beseeched Teresa to take the child to a healer so that he could perform a ceremony to call back the baby's soul and cure her. Sensing her predicament, several women promised to save Teresa's place in line, stating that upon her return, the doctors would probably be ready to see her grandchild. At the encouragement of the women, Teresa quickly left the hospital with the child in search of the healer. The man recommended was not home, and, unable to find anyone else, Teresa returned to the hospital. Upon her arrival and to her despair, the child had already passed away.

The doctor I interviewed that day told me the child had died of severe dehydration and fever. She was extremely frustrated at the nurses for not detecting the severity of this particular child's case. Indeed, dehydration was among the top causes of infant mortality in Bolivia, and there had been great effort to curtail this ailment through public-health campaigns, education, and the ready availability of oral rehydration therapies. Later that afternoon I mentioned this story to Flora, one of the women I came to know best throughout my fieldwork. I was quite saddened by the events and upset that the nurses had not attended to the grandmother and child sooner. I told Flora what the doctors told me: the child had died of dehydration. She corrected me with strong conviction: "No María, it was not dehydration. That child died of susto. A child with susto does not last more than twenty-four hours without a healer's treatment."

Flora's unwavering certainty in the diagnosis of susto somewhat surprised me, given the intensity of education campaigns against gastrointestinal diseases implemented in the region. Flora had regularly gone to seek care from medical doctors (as well as local healers) for herself and for her children, and, naively, I thought she would "believe" the doctors diagnosis. Yet the sureness with which she corrected my interpretation was a ready reminder of the extent to which "traditional" health beliefs about illness and emotions were vibrant and shaped the way people formulated their healing strategies. It was also evidence of the way individuals interpreted how the "global" affected the "local" and how far-removed factors beyond many people's control became intimately embodied into numerous illnesses and symptoms. The child's case of susto was not by any means a "new" illness that emerged in response to the presence of the U.S. Drug Enforcement Agency in the area. But as places undergo rapid change, new elements become integrated and entangled into people's lives and infuse their understandings of illness and distress. In this particular case, the war on drugs and this relatively new element in their environment—the army jets—came to be seen as a cause of this folk illness.

This book approaches emotion narratives as productive arenas from which to explore how the intimate experiences of illness and distress are linked to what medical anthropologists call "social suffering"—the broad array of social and structural conditions that underlie human anguish and misery (Kleinman, Das, and Lock 1997). When human suffering takes the form of an illness or symptom, whether it be cancer or susto, there is more to that experience that just the pathophysiology of cell proliferation or dehydration. Anthropologists have tried to address how patients and their caretakers "experience the social significance and moral meaning of their physical afflictions, material deprivation and loss" (Wilkinson 2004, 114). In many parts of Bolivia, expressed and unexpressed emotions are at the heart of various illnesses and symptoms. This book thus probes the emotional and intersubjective constructs that shape the social dramas through which people live as they struggle to cope with shifting economic, political, moral, and intimate landscapes (Biehl, Good, and Kleinman 2007b, 10). Teresa was left with the responsibility of raising her granddaughter while her daughter and son-in-law migrated to Argentina in search of more reliable sources of income than could be secured by growing carnations and potatoes on their small farm. Teresa was caught between her own beliefs about the role emotions played in the onset of illness and her daughter's ambivalence about such beliefs and faith deposited in "modern" medicine. As Teresa juggled these competing knowledge bases, she tried to secure the best possible care for her granddaughter.

The stories that unfold in the following pages occurred at important junctures in Bolivia's political and economic history. During the late 1990s, when the bulk of the fieldwork for this book was conducted, Bolivia was in the midst of a series of drastic economic reforms that were intended to modernize the economy and were backed by the International Monetary Fund (IMF). Simultaneously, the country (one of the world's top producers of coca leaves) was also a focal point of the U.S.-backed war on drugs. Although the implementation of economic reforms significantly halted rampant inflation rates, it did so upon the shoulders of the poor. What resulted was not economic opportunity, the alleviation of poverty, or a sense of security and hope but rather more distress and uncertainty. This distress was embodied in numerous ways, and the narratives in this book speak not only to intersubjective suffering but also to larger political, economic, and social issues affecting the region.

Political Restructuring and Embodied Manifestations of Distress

Since the 1990s, when Bolivia made headlines in the American press, often featured were massive popular protests drawing together thousands of citizens across class and ethnic lines. These demonstrations helped annul exploitative contracts with transnational corporations, prevent the privatization of numerous national industries, catalyze the resignation of politicians considered to serve corporate interests abroad over local needs, and in 2005 bring to power the country's first indigenous president, Evo Morales. Protestors often reacted to the implementation of what has commonly become known as neoliberal reforms. Since the late 1980s, Bolivia was an important testing ground for these economic policies, which included market liberalization and the decentralization of power (Kohl and Farthing 2006; Shultz and Draper 2008). Simultaneously, the nation also experienced another set of policies affecting the wider Andean regions: the war on drugs. As unemployment rates soared, the coca/cocaine industry and the informal economy surrounding it helped mitigate the economic costs of the austere neoliberal measures promoted by the IMF (Van Vleet 2008; García Argañarás 1997). Together these economic and political policies profoundly reconfigured people's aspirations, their self-identity, and the ways they related to one another, to their work, and to the state (Greenhouse, Mertz, and Warren 2002; Greenhouse 2010).

Economists heralded the IMF-backed initiatives as prerequisites to improve economic conditions and usher Bolivia (and other developing nations) more prominently into the global economy (Harvey 2005). Yet at the time of my fieldwork in the late 1990s the promises for a more prosperous economy, greater employment opportunities, and a more competitive edge in the global economy remained unfulfilled. The print and television media regularly displayed powerful visual images of thousands of shouting demonstrators, the militarization of cities, and the setting up of makeshift roadblocks capable of paralyzing the nation. These images, however, represent just one facet of the widespread dissatisfaction with the economic reforms implemented.

In this book I look at a different form of protest from the perspective of Punata, a small town nestled in an area known as the Valle Alto, the high valley in the heart of the Bolivian Andes. I argue that, in Bolivia's hesitant courtship with globalization, the turmoil around the political and economic situation

Map 1. Map of Bolivia

was also manifested in the visceral and emotional dis-ease experienced by many women. I examine the dissatisfaction with widespread economic instability from the vantage point of Quechua- and Spanish-speaking market- and working-class women and the everyday struggles they confronted in their search for well-being and "tranquility." I take emotions and the embodied manifestations of distress as a window through which to observe the effects of social suffering and the subtle articulations between the political restructuring of the state and the private anxieties women experienced under enduring economic and political volatility.

During my fieldwork I could detect that, aside from the frequent mass protests that occurred in the capital and larger cities, protest on a much smaller scale also unfolded as people complained and embodied what Nancy Scheper-Hughes and others have called the violences of everyday life, an expanded notion of what constitutes "violence" including: the lack of jobs, of money, and of hope for a prosperous future (Scheper-Hughes 1992a; Kleinman, Das, and Lock 1997). Scheper-Hughes argues that everyday violence can interweave itself so subtly into the social, political, and economic fabric of a place that it is rendered invisible, taken for granted, and even seen as normal. In Punata, everyday violence was manifested in the headaches and "pained hearts" of market women, in episodes of domestic violence experienced in some marriages, in the "normal" bouts of diarrhea experienced by infants or the general malaise that people complained about. While many of the symptoms that women voiced were not always or necessarily life threatening, they could be debilitating and were a daily reminder of the distress experienced in difficult economic times. Such symptoms, manifested in women or in their family members, prevented them from feeling *tranquilas*—tranquil, at peace, or at ease—and signaled tensions in the social landscape. The ailments were often a physical manifestation of social suffering: distress caused by poverty, domestic violence, the disillusionment of having social (and even family) networks fail or other indignities and hardships produced by the economic reforms. Thus, symptoms were a way for the distressed to give voice to an altered relationship to the world and to others (Biehl and Moran-Thomas 2009, 267). I approach the women's narratives as constituting the local knowledge that shaped their own understandings of health and well-being.

Society's enduring ethnic, class, and gendered power structures, as well as economic and political factors, extend their reach to shape people's experience of the world around them. However, even within the constraints posed by these larger structures, people consciously made choices in their lives and grappled with the injustices they witnessed, or even helped perpetuate, in their day-to-day existence. This book seeks to capture a variety of women's experiences and their interpretations of how the emotions and ailments that affected them and their loved ones were shaped by the personal, historical, and economic contingencies through which they lived.

Defining Neoliberalism

Numerous social scientists have grappled with what is meant by neoliberalism (Harvey 2005; Ong 2006; Tsing 2005). I approach neoliberalism as a transnational project with political, social, and moral dimensions and a set of policies endorsed by supranational institutions (such as the IMF and the World Bank) that rely on the market to structure social interactions and economic activities. The neoliberal economic model rests on a number of important assumptions regarding the relationships between the state and the larger global community, and between the state and the individual. Proponents of neoliberalism hold an unwavering faith in the power of market forces to stimulate and develop economies. Thus, when markets are allowed to self-regulate and conditions are set up to allow entrepreneurship to thrive, countries are empowered to compete in the global economy, or so the theory goes. Developing economies are thus encouraged to shift their "inward oriented" strategies to achieve self-sufficiency (through the protection of weak national industries by imposing high import taxes, for example) to a more "outward oriented" approach in which free trade enables the integration of developing countries into the world market (Phillips 1998, ix; Kohl and Farthing 2009).

A shift also takes place with regard to the type of relationship an individual should have to the state. Too much state interference is seen as a negative force that threatens individual freedoms. Indeed "freedoms" are at the core of neoliberal governmentalities: "freedom of the market, freedom to buy and sell, the free exercise of property rights, freedom of discussion, possible freedom of expression" (Foucault in Cotoi 2011, 114). By emphasizing individual autonomy, flexibility, and choice, neoliberalism calls for a retrenchment of both state activities and the provision of social services, thus transferring these responsibilities to the private sector and to individuals themselves. Such shifts privilege an ethics in which individuals are self-enterprising and responsible for helping themselves rather than relying solely on external help (Lind 2002, 241; Ong 2006).

Neoliberalism, as an ideology and as a set of entrenched global policies, has several defining features and goals.[1] Chief among these is that there should be minimal regulation and that state-owned enterprises should be privatized. The rationale for privatization is that privately owned companies are more likely to rein in excesses and inefficiencies and are able to respond to the fluctuations and demands of markets and allocate resources in more productive ways than publicly owned enterprises (Kohl and Farthing 2006, 105). Furthermore, for economies to open to international capital, trade needs to be liberalized and regulatory barriers eliminated. As neoliberal economic models were implemented, there was also a radical retrenchment of social benefits. While enthusiasts of neoliberal economic approaches believe that following these steps and enacting tax reforms (such as cutting tax rates on overseas investments) attracts foreign investment and stimulates economic growth, skeptics raise concerns about the social and economic costs such policies have on local life-ways (see Kohl and Farthing 2006, 20; Phillips 1998).

While the ideology of neoliberalism across the globe may share a number of tenets, the local unfolding of this transnational project and reactions to it take on different configurations, depending on the historical, political, economic, social, and cultural features of a particular place and its relationship to the global economy (Ong 2006). Individual countries face different challenges and opportunities as policies and recommendations are set in place, reminding us that neoliberalism is not a homogeneous project (Phillips 1998, xvii; Lind 2002). Indeed, over the span of twenty-five years, Bolivia, the "poster child" for the implementation of neoliberal policies during the 1980s, metamorphosed into the "poster child" for the antiglobalization movement, as powerful popular protests challenged and in some cases rescinded some of the contracts established through the implementation of the new economic plan (Kohl and Farthing 2009, 72). Dissatisfaction with the implementation of the policies, as mentioned earlier, was expressed not only on the streets of Bolivia's major cities but also more intimately, at the level of the body.

Ethnography, aptly called "the science of contextualization" (Greenhouse 2010, 2), with its attention to the intricacies of social life and social relations, is a powerful tool that helps dismantle many of the generalizations we make about neoliberalism and can help us understand how families were affected on the ground. In the chapters that follow I examine a few of the ways neoliberalism unfolded in Bolivia. Through attention to the emotion narratives of women, I seek to explore what the repercussions of neoliberalism have been for the poor. What helped attenuate the initial effects of these reforms? What larger structural, economic, and political factors help us contextualize the embodied distress experienced by women and children? How did the reforms affect people's abilities to earn a living, and in what ways were their social relations stressed? Finally, how do emotion narratives help us trace the shapes social suffering has taken in Bolivia?

Emotions, Failing Socialities, and the Body

In order to understand the links between larger structural, economic, and political factors affecting people's lives and their well-being in Punata, I argue that one must be cognizant of the ways people conceptualize emotions, sociality, and the body. As in all places across the world, the body and the illnesses and distress affecting it are profoundly "social" (Biehl, Good, and Kleinman 2007a; Kleinman, Das, and Lock 1997; Lock and Farquhar 2007). That is to say, in addition to the biological factors that can unleash illness, circumstances such as faulty social relations, the stresses of unemployment or underemployment, social inequalities, fragmented families, violence among intimates, among others, are a common denominator for many ailments. More important, in Punata emotions in response to these social and economic factors—feelings of rage, sorrow, pining for loved ones, desire for things beyond one's economic reach, fright, and envy—are considered intricately linked to numerous illnesses and symptoms. Julie Livingston, a historian who works in Africa and relies on oral histories to reconstruct the Tswana history and anthropology of the human body, echoes similar findings when she asserts: "There was no way to understand medicine or vernacular forms of embodiment without also grappling with the cultural norms of emotional continence and expression as aspects of medicine and public health" (Livingston in Eustace et al. 2012, 1489). Indeed, the women I worked with at once talked about their physical and emotional distress, making it difficult to tease apart emotion from many "folk" illnesses (Cartwright 2007; Rebhun 1993, 1994). Talk of emotions/illness reveals insights into the subjective experience of how globalization was felt in Bolivia by poor and aspiring middle-class women and their children and what it was like to live in a country undergoing radical economic reforms (see also Comaroff and Comaroff 2001).

The political and economic changes happening in Bolivia during the 1990s and in the first years of the twenty-first century profoundly affected everyday life and interactions between intimates and acquaintances. In this process, moral and ethical worlds were also reconfigured, challenging the very basic rules of sociality that people took for granted (Das and Kleinman 2000; Parsons 2013). For example, the ethical principles and values underpinning the neoliberal agenda placed a greater focus on individual responsibility and individual freedom (Harvey 2005; Comaroff and Comaroff 2001). Indeed, proponents of neoliberalism argue that untethering individual entrepreneurial aspirations and supporting them with an institutional context that privileges strong private-property rights, free markets, and free trade is the best path to advance human well-being (see Harvey 2005, 2). The Bolivian state in the 1990s was very much seduced by the promises of this economic approach but overlooked the ways the ethical values heralded by the economic reforms implemented were pitted against more "traditional" values of reciprocal exchange that dated back generations (Allen 1988; Van Vleet 2008; Weismantel 1988). Furthermore, opportunities to *avanzar*, advance oneself, were not equally accessible to all (Van Vleet 2008). The reforms increased the economic disparities between different social sectors and in many ways strained relations between extended kin, gender relations in the home, and social relations among neighbors.

Much of the emotional distress I heard voiced by women was related to social conflicts, domestic violence, economic scarcity, and what might be better understood as "failed sociality."[2] Failed sociality occurs when familiar networks of support become faulty and unpredictable, or when people are unable to meet the social, emotional, and economic expectations placed on them (Ferguson 1999, 2006; Tapias 2006b; Taussig 1987). In social contexts where prosperity and success were unevenly and undemocratically experienced, a slow but steady erosion of trust occurred that reshaped how people behaved toward one another (Greenhouse 2010; Das and Kleinman 2000). In Punata, failed sociality and social suffering were embodied and seen to negatively affect one's emotional and physical well-being. The "medical" discourses of embodied social suffering that my interlocutors drew upon centered not only on numerous folk illnesses, which included susto, *arrebato*, *Pachamama*, and *aire*, but also on a range of symptoms, including headaches, *sonqo nanay* (a pained heart that causes general malaise), vomiting, debility and loss of strength, bouts of bad luck and misfortune caused by the envy of others, facial and partial bodily paralysis, infant diarrhea, and numerous other symptoms. When asked what caused their own or their children's symptoms and illnesses, women regularly pointed to emotions.

Andrea, for example, told me her husband had come home drunk one night and beat her during an argument. She later breastfed her son and within a few hours his nails, mouth, and feet became purple and he experienced heavy diarrhea. When asked what happened, Andrea said the child got *arrebato*, an illness in which a mother's sorrow or anger is transmitted through her milk making it "poisonous" and resulting in severe diarrhea or even the child's death if not properly treated.

Ana, a local market woman and single mother, took her nine-year-old son to the city market. Upon returning home he began vomiting. When I asked what caused his illness, she explained it had been *deseo*, desire: "He craved fruit in the market, but I didn't have money to buy his wish, so he got sick." She no longer took him on her excursions to the city to restock her stall.

Justina tied a red piece of tattered string around her two-year-old niece's wrist to help rid her of the symptoms of *tirisya*, a folk illness that causes general listlessness and lethargy. This folk illness results from a child's sadness, longing, and pining for an absent loved one. A few weeks earlier, the child had been left behind by her parents who migrated to Argentina for work.

Flora, another market vendor, could not recover from joint pain and swollen limbs despite the medical treatment she received from a physician in the city. Concurrently, Flora went to a local healer who read her fortune in coca leaves and told her that in addition to contracting *Pachamama*, a folk illness that occurs when rage or sorrow is expressed in particular sacred spaces, she had been ensorcelled by a coworker envious of her economic prosperity.

Finally, let us take the case of Rosalía, a thirty-two-year-old Bolivian hospital cleaning woman who had a heated argument with and was verbally abused by one of the doctors on staff. Fearful that arguing back might entail the loss of her needed job, Rosalía held in her anger and three hours later fainted and experienced *aire*, a partial paralysis of her body. After telling me that her symptoms had been caused by rage, I asked, "What else?" to which she replied, "That was it, I felt anger."

In the context of Bolivia, the stories people tell about their emotions, symptoms, and illnesses are an index of their social situations, relations, and conflicts, and they illustrate that "failures of the body . . . [are also] failures of one's social world" (Das and Das 2007, 69). When women tell stories about the emotions they express or conceal, their reasons for doing so, the concerns they have for their own or their children's health, the therapeutic interventions they seek, or the issues and situations they view as "risky," they very much tell a story that speaks to cultural domains of power. What one expresses, whom one is able to express emotions to, and what is at stake in such expression is very much related to power relations and powerlessness. Maynes, Pierce, and Laslett, whose interdisciplinary work focuses on the value of personal narratives, aptly remind us that individual life stories are continuously "expressed in culturally specific forms; read carefully, they provide unique insights into the connections between individual life trajectories and collective forces and institutions beyond the individual" (2008, 3).

Social Suffering, Subjectivity, and Emotions

Several interrelated bodies of literature influence my interpretation of the emotion narratives presented in the following pages: the anthropological scholarship examining social suffering and new ways to analyze subjectivity and the anthropology of emotions.

The origin of illnesses and symptoms that occur cross-culturally cannot solely be limited to the pathogens that attack a body. A plethora of other social and political processes make individuals vulnerable to suffering—factors that often reflect social inequalities based on race, class, and gender. The body and suffering thus are not independent of social relations and social forces but continuously constituted by them (Kleinman, Das, and Lock 1997; Turner 1994). In considering an individual's biography of suffering, it is necessary to anchor it to the particularities of their social relations and to larger historical, political, and cultural contexts (Farmer 1996; see also Das 1996; Kleinman, Das, and Lock 1997; Scheper-Hughes 1992a). Suffering, argues Farmer, is "'structured' by historically given (and often economically driven) processes and forces that conspire—whether through routine, ritual or, as is more commonly the case, the hard surfaces of life—to constrain agency" (Farmer 2005, 40; see also Farmer 1996; Petryna 2002; Scheper-Hughes 1992a). These social and economic forces limit the choices that individuals can make on a day-to-day basis and can negatively affect health and well-being.

While understanding biological, social, political, and economic factors are crucial to formulate a more complete analysis of illnesses and symptoms, this approach alone can often push intimate details and contingencies that unfold in people's lives (which are so intrinsically linked to emotions) to blind spots within an ethnography. Undertaking a meaningful anthropology of affliction thus requires close examination of local knowledge, for it makes intelligible to others the way people's social dramas and experiences unfold. For the particular cases that are developed in this book, I draw attention to how Quechua- and Spanish-speaking market- and working-class women conceptualize well-being, their bodies, and emotions, and how these conceptualizations are intrinsically linked to interactions between community members and larger economic and political factors beyond many people's control. Such an approach helps bridge larger structural factors to the subjective experience of suffering and the meanings people ascribe to such suffering. João Biehl and others, for example, examine how intimate inner processes are "reshaped amid economic and political reforms, violence and social suffering" (Biehl, Good, and Kleinman 2007b, 1). They critique social-scientific and humanistic descriptions of illness, which may be mindful of the way bodies and health are shaped by biological, political, and social processes yet remain relatively "thin" in making the significance of lived experience more palpable (Biehl, Good, and Kleinman 2007a; Das and Das 2007). Similarly, Biehl, Good, and Kleinman (2007b) note the generalist quality that writings on illness exhibit, as if the broad cultural understandings that people share and the wider political and economic context in which people live suffice to understand people's experiences of an illness. Such an approach often sacrifices an understanding of how illness experiences are intrinsically textured and nuanced.

My examination of individual cases that occurred over the course of my fieldwork seeks to capture the depth of people's personhood as vulnerable individuals who experience difficulties, disappointments, tensions, and inconsistencies but who also resist, negotiate, and persevere in their search for well-being. The narratives evoked through my interviews allow me to explore not only how emotions are perceived to be linked to numerous illnesses but also how women intimately experienced these emotions and the particular contexts in which they have unraveled, shedding light on the conflicts and hardship faced in their day-to-day lives. Narratives of emotions thus provide a fruitful arena from which to glean the vulnerabilities brought about by political, economic, and social changes (see Boellstorff and Lindquist 2004 for special *Ethnos* issue on emotions in Southeast Asia). In my efforts to elucidate the emotional and illness experiences of women in Punata, I take seriously Andrew Beatty's call for a narrative approach to emotions (2010, 2013). As Beatty insightfully points out, "Emotions are not the creation of a moment; they participate in manifold relationships formed over periods of time" (2010, 430). Emotions, then, have a "past," a "history" embedded in and contingent upon prior events and related to a particular set of social relations. While Beatty is correct to assert that standard ethnographic representations, reliant on static case studies, often fail to elucidate the complexities of emotions, I would add that the extended fieldwork in which anthropologists engage puts us in a privileged position to be mindful of not only what Beatty calls the "historical emplotment of emotions" (2010, 432) but also their cultural emplotment. To trace out this cultural emplotment, I argue that a meaningful ethnography of emotions and affliction must examine the discursive, embodied, and performed dimensions of emotions (Escandell and Tapias 2010; Tapias 2006b; Tapias and Escandell 2011).

During the past three decades the anthropological interest in emotions has paralleled an increased interest in the body as a category of analysis. As the non-universality of Western medical notions of the body and illness have become truisms of medical anthropology (Csordas 1990, 1994; Farquar and Lock 2007; Lock 1993; Martin 1987; Scheper-Hughes and Lock 1987; Taussig 1980), the scholarship on emotions has also questioned the "universality" of emotions (Kitayama and Markus 1994; Lutz and White 1986). Extensive scholarship and several ethnographies have provided some outstanding examinations of the cross-cultural meanings, constructs, and "translatability" of emotion terms (Beatty 2005; Escandell and Tapias 2010; Geertz 1973; Good 2004; Lutz 1986, 1988; Padilla et al. 2008; Rebhun 1999; Rosaldo 1980; Tapias and Escandell 2011); emotions and their relationship to personhood (Desjarlais 1992; Rosaldo 1984); social relations and agency (Lutz and White 1986; Lyon and Barbalet 1994); and the sociopolitical dimensions of emotions (Abu-Lughod and Lutz 1990; Appadurai 1990; de Jong and Reis 2010; Van Vleet 2002, 2008).

In this book, I view emotions as processes that are not "natural" or "pre-cultural" (even though these emotions may very much feel natural and internal) but rather as profoundly shaped by the cultural context in which they occur and as phenomena that have local meanings and effects (Abu-Lughod and Lutz 1990b; Lutz 1986, 1988; Rebhun 1993, 1994; Rosaldo 1984; Scheper-Hughes 1992a; Tapias 2006a, 2006b). An analogy to language brings clarity to this approach: while humans are born with the ability to learn language, we are, in fact, "taught" language, and the languages we learn cross-culturally are distinct. Similarly, although we have bodies that experience emotions, those emotions are not the same everywhere: they may have different meanings, manifestations, or features.[3] Following in line with the seminal work of Lutz and Abu-Lughod (1990), I argue that emotions must be understood as aspects of sociality and social relations rather than as natural, internal biological states.

One strong criticism to the constructivist approach has centered on concerns that such an analysis has the potential to portray emotions as monolithic and as collective generalizations that belie the vibrant heterogeneity of individual experiences in a particular cultural setting (Reddy 1999). This view, however, can be addressed by the examination of how power relations intersect with emotional expression. Drawing inspiration from the work of Foucault, I highlight the discursive dimensions of emotions and place emphasis on how power structures influence their expression (Foucault 1978, 1981; see also Abu-Lughod and Lutz 1990; Appadurai 1990). Furthermore, non-essentialist feminist theory provides tools for further refining constructivism by demonstrating how individuals negotiate, orchestrate, and perform their emotional expression (Rebhun 1993, 1999; Tapias 2006b). In addition, a focus on the "performance" of emotions grants us insight into how, in everyday practice, people make decisions about what they can or want to "externalize" to others. In many instances, people may not be able to express their emotions, especially if it places them in a vulnerable position.

Some scholars are cautious about Foucault's discursive approach, with its emphasis on how societal power is inscribed on bodies. Chief among their unease: the method's inability to address bodies as social agents and for its lack of recognition of the role emotion plays in social life (Lyon and Barbalet 1994, 49). These authors draw from the literature on embodiment that has also proliferated within the sphere of medical and psychological anthropology (Csordas 1990, 1994; Lock 1993; Maschia-Lees 2011). This approach emphasizes that an understanding of culture should begin with an examination of the lived-in body (because one knows, feels, and thinks about the social world through the body) and an appreciation of the fact that "the" body is not a static standard: bodies are gendered, dynamic, and changing as they traverse the life cycle. In addition, people not only experience and carry their daily activities from within their bodies but also relate to other bodies. Similarly, I argue that people are not passive receptors of the dictates of social power. As people interact with others in their social milieu, emotions guide and prepare subjects for social action and enable an expression of agency, even if (as mentioned above) that agency initially entails not outwardly expressing emotions or taking action at all.

Lyon and Barbalet argue that emotions not only are embodied but also are the mediating factor between the body and the social world. Emotion, they propose, is the "experience of embodied sociality" (1994, 48). Authors who focus on the discursive aspects of emotion recognize that emotions are also embodied experiences that involve the whole person. Following their assertion that "emotion can be studied as embodied discourse only after its social and cultural—its discursive—character has been fully accepted" (Abu-Lughod and Lutz 1990, 13), this book emphasizes the need to attend to both dimensions. As I examine emotions in Punata, the above-mentioned approaches are coupled with a consideration of who holds power to express emotion, what emotions can be expressed and under what circumstances, and how emotions are experienced in the body.

With few exceptions, the scholarship on emotions and illness in Bolivia or the wider Andean region is fairly limited (see Hammer 1997). Some scholars have examined individual emotions and their effect on health (see Tousignant [1984] for sorrow in Ecuador; Alba [1989] for "pining" in Bolivia), and others have contributed to the extensive literature on nerves, susto (fright), and envy in Latin America (Davis and Low 1989a; Finnerman 1989a; Rebhun 1993;

Rubel 1984; Scheper-Hughes 1992a; Taussig 1987). In order to understand the social/emotional suffering of women and their attempts to both alleviate and to prevent their own suffering and that of their children, we need to make sense of the embodiment of emotions and the conceptual framework that shapes talk about emotion and illness simultaneously.

The Genesis of a Project

Since the late 1960s anthropologists have increasingly called for a more conscious reflection and analysis of the social position of the anthropologist, problematizing in the process the supposed objectivity and neutrality of the anthropological observer (Behar and Gordon 1992). Anthropologists turned the analytical lens on themselves to shed light on the partiality of the texts they create (Clifford 1986), the authority with which they write of the 'other' (Clifford 1983), and the discipline's lack of attention to the effects of colonialism and how early anthropology was complicit with structures of inequality engendered by colonial expansion (Asad 1973). Furthermore, they called for a more explicit examination of how the projects we pursue, the questions we ask, the relationships we form in the field, and the data we collect are intrinsically shaped by who we are, where we are in our lifecycles, and other aspects of our personal histories (Abu-Lughod 1993; Narayan 1993). While some have raised concerns about making the ethnographic endeavor too much about the anthropologist, others caution that the focus on representation can have the unintended result of paralyzing the researcher from his or her responsibility to take ethical and political stands in the face of injustice (Scheper-Hughes 1995). Critiques notwithstanding, it has become *de rigueur* in anthropology for writers to be reflexive and provide an understanding of how projects emerge.

In the interest of such reflexivity, I can say that my attraction to Bolivia began long before my first anthropology class. My parents and brothers immigrated to the United States from Bolivia in 1959; seven years later I was born in Queens, New York. Although I grew up hearing relatives reminisce about family, friends, and food, complain about politicians, and long for the spectacular landscapes of the Andes, my first visit to the country did not occur until I was twenty-three years old, when I accompanied my mother to re-visit her homeland. It was this first trip that catalyzed the change in my career plans from medical school to graduate school in medical anthropology. As I traveled through rural areas in Bolivia, I wondered how millions of dollars funneled into health development programs could have such little effect in a country ravaged by some of the highest infant mortality rates in the Americas. I felt anthropology might be able to help me answer these questions.

When I began fieldwork, my familial connection to Bolivia and my situation in life opened many doors. Being female, single, and childless proved to be significant with regard to the relationships and interactions I was able to forge in the field. For reasons that I will explain shortly, I carried out my study in the central market, a heavily gendered environment. It was not seen as out of the ordinary for me, a woman, to spend countless hours there—something that would have been viewed with suspicion had I been male. As a single woman I was also "looked after," fed and incorporated into many people's family lives. Finally, as someone without children, my questions about childrearing, caretaking, breastfeeding, or mothering were answered with great patience and not treated as naïve but rather as coming from someone who did not have experience.[4]

My interest in different ways of healing and understanding the body cross-culturally has also been longstanding. From the time I could barely see over tabletops I can remember seeing my grandmother pouring hot water over a strainer. Yaya, as we called her, was a great believer in the medicinal powers of plants. Anise tea was good for stomachaches, *cola de caballo* was a diuretic, and nothing helped menstrual cramps like *yerba luisa*. Similarly, when I fell ill with a life-threatening anemia at age ten, my parents did not hesitate to pursue all the health options before them. Not only did I have a bone marrow transplant in the United States, but my father, who at the time was teaching in Brazil, also procured the advice of a "naturalist" who recommended an alternative treatment for my anemia that I followed as well.[5] Perhaps it is not surprising, then, that as graduate student I became increasingly interested in understanding how people sought out healing during a health crisis based on local concepts of medicines, the body, and illness.

I chose to conduct my fieldwork in the provincial town of Punata, located an hour away from Cochabamba, one of the main cities in the country. In the late 1990s, Punata was a dusty market town of thirteen thousand people located in the Valle Alto, a once very fertile valley. Infant mortality rates were approximately seventy deaths per one thousand births, and from a biomedical perspective the main health problems affecting the population included respiratory illnesses, infectious diseases, traumas, accidental chemical and food poisoning, and gastrointestinal and parasite problems (Secretaría Nacional de Salud 1996). Both Quechua and Spanish were spoken in most households (70.9 percent of the population was bilingual). At the time of my extended fieldwork, the average household was made of thick adobe bricks, plastered and covered with a tin or tile roof. Most houses had an inner courtyard or garden, where domestic activities such as washing and the preparation of meals took place. Municipal water was provided for eight hours a day to 58.3 percent of households, although water pressure and availability varied throughout town. Wealthier homes had water pumps and were thus provided with water all day. Eighty-eight percent of households had electricity, and 40 percent had bathroom facilities in the form of latrines or toilets (Census data, 1992, Province Punata, vol. 123). Remittances from Spain in the early years of the twenty-first century, however, changed the architectural face of town, providing them with modern comforts found in any metropolitan city, as I illustrate in the final chapter of this book.

When you are a novice anthropologist who is slightly shy, as I was when I began this project, the initial stages of research can be fraught with fieldwork jitters (Hume and Mulcock 2004). Each day I'd go around town "visiting" people, chatting, listening, and engaging in what sometimes felt like shameless lurking. I had difficulty effectively explaining to people what I was supposed to do as a participant observer. When people would see me in the streets or in the market, they'd smile and kindly ask "*¿Paseando señorita?*" "Going for a stroll, Miss?" I'd smile back, not quite knowing what to say and think: "Yes, I'm strolling around, but I'm strolling profoundly." Strolling profoundly, a variation of "deep hanging out," was helping me get a sense of the people in town. As I tried to figure out how people were related, what people did for a living, what they did during the day, and what they did for leisure, I was trying to learn about social life in Punata. Doña Eustaquia, an elderly, spirited market woman who sold coca leaves and who was conscious of the privileges of *gringos* and *gringas*, was not so diplomatic. One day as she saw me perambulating in town she said, irritated: "*Señorita, usted se pasa el día visitando la gente y hablando. Dime, ¿cuando trabaja usted?*" "Miss, you spend the whole day visiting people and talking. Tell me, *when* do you work?" And before I could answer, she continued on her way, leaving me defensively thinking, "I AM working." But what was this "work" I was trying to accomplish?

When I first arrived in Punata, I approached the local hospital for support with my project. However, while it was very valuable to visit local communities with healthcare workers, attend reproductive health workshops, observe vaccination campaigns, hang out at the hospital, and converse with doctors and patients, I was always concerned that people would tell me only one side of their stories: the biomedical side. Each day, before going to the hospital, I'd stop by the central market to purchase food for the midday meal. Like many women in Punata, I did not own a refrigerator, so a daily trip to the market was a necessity. I found a lot of comfort in the market: it was lively,

Figure 1. Morning at the market

colorful, and people were friendly. The market was centrally located and, like other provincial markets in Cochabamba, was housed in a square structure with an inner courtyard. In this courtyard women laid their colorful woven awayos down on the floor, displaying their strategically stacked produce on it: fava beans, fruit, tomatoes, hot peppers, corn, potatoes, spices, flowers, canned goods, gifts, and other household items. There, I'd converse and joke with the market women, and I'd find myself spending more and more of my morning in that setting, delaying my routine visits to the hospital. I'd hang around and listen to the interactions between the market women and their *caseras*, their "regulars."[6]

I had not intended to work with market women when I first started my fieldwork, but I realized very quickly that the market was "gossip central." There was not a day that passed when matters related to emotions, health, social conflicts, or illness were not discussed. Caseras gave each other advice about their symptoms and shared home remedies and names of healers or good doctors in the city. Women also passed judgment on one another, and regular, hushed conversations centered on how *this* woman was mistreated by her husband, or on the poor job *that* woman was doing raising her son. Market women commented on who was sick, who had died, or how that little old lady who lived near the plaza was ensorcelled by her daughter-in-law. During this daily gossip, women encouraged each other to reflect on the conflicts they had, on whether they owed money and how this could affect their health, or whether they got angry or frightened in particular spots in the landscape.

The conversations in the market were richly detailed and debated, not stifled, as they had been in the hospital. The informality of the market allowed me to talk with women about my interests in health, their jobs, and events in town. They would also ask me about my family, why I was not married yet, what I was doing so far away from home, and what life was like in the United States. Although the women I interacted with knew I was in Punata to do a study, during the first months of my fieldwork I never asked direct questions about health. Although the topic came up spontaneously frequently, I was cautious about prying for too much intimate information in public settings and also wanted people to get to know me. When, at last, I decided people knew me well enough (and I was over my initial fieldwork apprehensions) for me to conduct more in-depth interviews, I was somewhat surprised by one woman's response to my request: "Of course! We were wondering when you were going to get started!" People readily granted me interviews and invited me to visit them. At that point, I realized my lurking had paid off. The more in-depth conversations and interviews took place in numerous settings. Sometimes they took place in the market, but more commonly they took place in the privacy of people's homes. More formal interviews were recorded, but often the "historical baggage" that particular emotions carried emerged in informal interactions and in stories and gossip women told me about themselves, neighbors, and family members. These stories were written up in field notes and served as valuable contextualizing anchors to the life narratives I collected. I also conducted participant observation in numerous other sites as well, including the regional Tuesday market (*feria*), a healthcare development project sponsored by the GTZ (a German funding agency), a Catholic youth center, and corn beer halls known locally as *chicherías*.

The weekly feria of Punata played a very important role regionally, as it articulated communities scattered throughout the Valle Alto as people convened to sell, exchange, and buy products. The presence of the regional market was one of the main reasons I chose to carry out my study in Punata. Not only did the commercial activity and exchange each week render the town vibrant, but it was also a very dynamic town in terms of its healthcare facilities and options. The *feria del Martes*, as it is known locally, attracted people not only from all over the Valle Alto and Cochabamba but also from places as far away as Mizque, seven hours away by bus. On Tuesdays, the chaos, dust, noise, smells of food wafting through the air, and confusion gives Punata the flavor of a much larger city than it was in actuality. Sales, purchases, and bartering took place in the stalls that lined the streets of the feria or from the wheelbarrows of itinerant sellers who wandered the streets. The feria played a pivotal role in the local formal and informal economy; transportation was available to every corner of the valley on Tuesdays, and hundreds of trucks, buses, vans, and taxis could be seen scattered throughout the town. The feria also attracted numerous healers, ritualists, and herb sellers. On Tuesdays, in addition to the presence of local healers, many others came from distant areas to attend to the crowds of patients who arrived each week to also sell their products. The significance of the feria as a major articulating place for the entire Valle Alto was not a fact overlooked by the GTZ, which funded an eleven-year healthcare project for the Valle Alto. Punata became the site of the main reference hospital and the project district offices. On any given Tuesday, the hospital waiting room, clinics, pharmacies, as well as the places where healers attended patients were packed, from 7 A.M. until nighttime.

The top priorities of the GTZ project included improving infrastructure of the Valle Alto (in terms of hospitals and health posts); training healthcare personnel (health promoters, nurse's aides, and native experts in health); implementing public-health campaigns; recording health statistics; improving water supplies; establishing infant, school-age, reproductive, and oral health programs; and setting up an essential-medicines program. Through the project I was able to observe activities at the hospital and visit satellite health posts. These visits allowed me to interview physicians and staff, sit in on consultations, observe interactions between doctors and patients, accompany nurses on vaccination campaigns, and travel with teams of doctors to remote villages in the hospital ambulance. I also attended some workshops on family planning and traditional medicine and sat in on administrative meetings.

Across the street from the hospital was the Centro Virgin del Rosario, operated by a group of Chilean and Spanish nuns. The nuns had established an educational center for women and offered classes in knitting, sewing, cooking, baking, secretarial skills, and word processing. Classes were held throughout the academic year in the afternoons and evenings; as many as two hundred students were enrolled during any particular term. The center gave me the opportunity to interact with a younger female population than those who visited the market. I spent a semester teaching English to the secretarial students and in this way met many of the women I later interviewed. Many of these women between ages sixteen and twenty-seven already had several children. Working with these women granted me insight into the preoccupations of young mothers and marital conflicts facing young couples.

I also observed interactions between people as they relaxed and got together to drink *chicha* (corn beer), either at family run chicherías (corn beer halls), in the market, or at various homes. It is truly difficult to understate the central social and economic role that chicha and chicherías play in Punata and the larger Andean area. The Lonely Planet Travel Guide to Bolivia (one of the most popular travel guides for tourists and backpackers) devotes a small paragraph to Punata. It begins: "The small market town of Punata, 48 kilometers east of Cochabamba, is known for the finest *chicha* in all Bolivia" (Swaney 1996, 346). Indeed, Punata is recognized nationwide as the chicha capital of Bolivia. There may be several chicherías on any random block in the heart of Punata. Chicha is very much a part of quotidian life and is one of the greatest sources of pride for locals. Known as the "Nectar of the Valley," no fiesta, celebration, or funeral is held without an ample supply of chicha.

Because I was in the field for two years, I was often able to accompany some women on their quests for healing—to appointments with doctors and healers, on a pilgrimage to Bombori, Potosí (see chapter 5), or to discuss medicines with pharmacists or diets with "naturalists." Because I was interested in the multiple discourses that emerge regarding health, emotions, and social conflict, I focused on these diverse sites because each produced different types of competing knowledge about the same health event. In addition, it was by interacting with others in these sites that I came to meet people I could interview.

After my extended fieldwork (1996 to 1998) I returned to Bolivia in 2003, 2006, and 2010. These trips were shorter, lasting from two to six weeks, and while there was often a feeling of "catching up" with friends, my particular interests during these trips tended to be more directed and focused on issues related to breastfeeding (see Tapias 2006a) and on how constructs of emotions had changed with migration. These latter questions have also taken me to Spain, where I have interviewed many migrants from Punata as well as other areas of Cochabamba. The concluding chapter provides a brief introduction to that project but remains very relevant to this book, as migration became one of the key strategies people deployed to sustain their families financially and to secure steadier sources of income. Suffering has taken on new shapes in Punata, but the emotional underpinnings of illnesses are still very much a part of the picture.

Layout of the Book

In my analysis of the articulation of global and structural factors with more intimate experiences of illness, I seek in this book to forefront people's experiences in their own words. In chapter 1, I present the social and cultural contexts in which the women featured in this book live. A key part of chapter 1 is a discussion of the neoliberal reforms that were implemented in Bolivia. The chapter considers the effects of these reforms and the economic strategies people deployed in order to make ends meet, such as international migration to Argentina, Spain, and other countries. I discuss the role of narco-trafficking in Punata, as numerous people sought employment in both coca-growing activities or the informal sector related to the cocaine trade.

In chapter 2, I examine the elusive and porous boundaries of the body among Punateños and Punateñas and explore the relationship between physicality and sociality. The chapter explores the conceptualizations people have about the "fluidity" of emotions and the predicaments inherent in the expression of emotions, larger Andean notions of corporeality, sociability, and the flow of substances between individuals.

The next three chapters are devoted to the narratives of several women to show how political and economic transformations were interlinked with everyday life, subjectivity, agency, and the experience of illnesses. Themes uniting the diverse narratives include how to negotiate injustice, loss, and changing social landscapes. Chapter 3 discusses the intergenerational embodiment of distress and examines how social suffering affects children through folk illnesses known as *arrebato* and *debilidad*. The cases are presented within the context of the global war on drugs and money-laundering activities that affected people at a local level. In chapter 4 I examine the uneven terrain of economic success in Punata. The relatively higher economic success of some market women had significant social and emotional costs. The chapter discusses envy and concerns about sorcery (and by extension ill health) and how women reconciled their economic ambitions with social expectations. I describe a religious pilgrimage to a remote town in the department of Potosí and devotion to an image known as Tata Bombori. Chapter 5 examines changing conceptualization of emotions and practices of secrecy as people migrate to Spain in search of better economic opportunities. In the Conclusion of the book, I reflect on how emotions constitute a fruitful site from which to examine the effects of globalization and the role they play in reconfiguring social relations. The Conclusion examines multiple attitudes toward the government of Evo Morales, whose presidency promised to dismantle the neoliberal agenda.

1

Neoliberalism on the Ground
Political, Economic, and Social Landscapes

Most mornings, it was not the strong Valle Alto sun streaming through my window that woke me. It was not the cacophonous chorus of neighborhood roosters, nor the gleeful chatter of children running off to school. It was not the squeaky wheels of carts hauling produce to the market three blocks from my house, the church bells calling the faithful to Mass at 7:00 A.M., or the incessant buzzing of my Casio alarm clock. What drew me out of sleep at dawn was the slow and rhythmic *swish-swish-swish* of Doña Soledad's broom sweeping the sidewalk right below my bedroom window.

Each day, regardless of season, the elderly neighbor—bundled in several layers, a full black *pollera* (the layered or pleated skirt worn by many native Andean women), and warm tights—swept with her *pichana*, a sheaf of dried and stiff prickly straw tied together with a little bit of string. She meticulously swept the debris off the sidewalk onto the dirt road, and when finished, she would issue my second wake-up call: the sound of water slapping onto the road. She cast her red bucket of water in a circular motion like a fine liquid net over the surface of the dirt and pebble road. This way, when trucks and cars came jostling down our unpaved street, they didn't leave behind a cloud of dust.

By 5 A.M. most people in Punata were already wide awake. Many women, like Doña Soledad, busily swept or watered the sidewalks and roads. Others prepared morning tea or cleaned their courtyards. Doña Selma, my landlady, blended the daily concoction of herbs she drank for her ulcer: *llanten*, bee pollen, and *pochongora*, with honey added to make it drinkable. When the academic year was in recess, Carina, a seventh-grader who lived a few doors down from me, was usually headed to her parents' fields to water the alfalfa and feed the few animals they owned. While her brothers slept in, Carina frequently complained she was expected not only to complete this chore but then also to return home and prepare the midday soup. Unlike her brothers, she eagerly awaited the start of the school year, when she was then relieved of these chores.

Doña Flora, who lived across town from me, was already washed up, had twisted her long graying hair and switches into two thick braids, donned her pollera, sweaters, apron, and butcher's hat, and prepared to go to the market to sell meat—something she did seven days a week all year-round, with the exception of Good Friday. Justino, the *campesino* hired to help transport Flora's meat to the market, waited outside her home with his wheelbarrow. All bundled up, he wore the flaps of his brown tattered alpaca hat hanging down around his ears. Flora's daughter Mariana, who lived across the cobblestoned street, tidied up her small convenience store (located in the front room of her home) to the sound of the latest *cumbias* and *chicha* music blaring from her radio and prepared breakfast for her two small sons, who normally ignored her first two wake-up calls. Her father, Juan, depending on when the water cooperative allotted him his share of water, could be watering his potato fields or, on Tuesday, the day of the regional market, purchasing cattle for slaughter.

Doña Vera, another market woman, was in the market before 4:30 A.M. preparing *tojori* and *api* (sweet hot beverages made from white and purple corn) for the customers who ate their first meal at her stall. Doña Wanda, up since 3:00 A.M., busily removed the last batches of bread from her oven and sent them to the market with her two helpers. Norma, a purveyor of peas and fava beans, began to collect the tiny trickle of water delivered from her spigot from 5:00 to 11:00 A.M. in numerous buckets.[1] While she waited, Norma could be either doing the family's laundry or peeling potatoes for the midday meal before heading to her market "stall," a colorful woven blanket spread out on the floor, shaded by a large white parasol stitched together from the fabric of old flour sacks.

By 6:00 A.M., as the sun rose, women would begin to arrive from all corners of town or neighboring villages to the market. They washed down the tile countertops, stalls, or floors and set up parasols that would offer protection from the parching midday sun. Once settled, many would go to one of the breakfast vendors and purchase something warm to drink and perhaps a fresh piece of bread, fried pieces of sweet dough (known as *buñuelos*), or a cheese-filled *empanada*. Those market women who had "contracts" with restaurant owners—usually sealed by *compadrazgo* ties (ritual kinship ties)—delivered meat, vegetables, or other products promptly so that the cooks could begin to simmer the midday meals. By 7:00 A.M. a steady trickle of customers would arrive at the market to buy their groceries. Since many Punateños lacked refrigerators, a daily trip to the market was one of the tasks housewives or daughters would undertake in the course of their day. Men were rarely sent to the market to buy items for the household because, according to most women, they lacked the "common sense" needed to buy quality and reasonably priced groceries.

Heading toward the plaza, past the "John Travolta" and the "Sting" barber and beauty shops, were the taxi-truffis[2] filled with passengers headed to Cochabamba. Some passengers would return later in the day after conducting business in the city, while many students attending university or women employed as domestic workers would return only on the weekend. Sandra, the newspaper seller, set up her stand with a large stack of the day's edition of *Los Tiempos*, the Cochabamba newspaper, shouting: "Tieeeeeemmpooooos!" Father Crecensio, the parish priest, would be saying Mass to the local Chilean nuns and a few faithful. The pharmacists in town cleaned off the dust from the counters at which they attended their clients and prepared to raise the corrugated metal door of their respective businesses. On the very edge of town, the nighttime staff was briefing the daytime crew at the hospital. Rosalía, depending on her shift as a hospital janitor, could either be on her way home or preparing to go to work.

The hustle and bustle characteristic of early mornings in Punata belied the fact that many families, in spite of working hard and trying to maximize their resources, were struggling to make ends meet in the face of the economic hardship the country faced during the late 1990s. Indeed, many did not experience the prosperity that the government had promised would materialize "in the long run" through the implementation of neoliberal reforms. In the unrestricted, competitive market economy promoted by neoliberalism, the playing field was not always level and the "losers" far outnumbered the "winners." Furthermore, in the daily activities with which people occupied themselves were hidden the more intimate and bodily ways people experienced the effects of neoliberal reforms.

In this chapter I explore how neoliberalism unfolded in the context of Bolivia and consider the economic strategies people deployed to help mitigate the effects of the reforms. As suggested above, not all in Punata prospered, although some did. The emergent inequalities strained the way people related to one another, altered relationships of power, and had effects on individuals regarding whom they could depend on and trust. Understanding these repercussions, however, also requires an understanding of the social and cultural contexts in which the women featured in this ethnography lived, and it is to that effort that the latter part of this chapter turns.

Neoliberalism in Bolivia

The international financial community has referred to the general lack of economic growth during the 1980s as the "lost decade" for many Latin American countries (Phillips 1998, xv). During this period Bolivia experienced strong economic decline and a persistent debt crisis. The gross national product during these years fell by almost 25 percent, and hyperinflation rates reached well over 20,000 percent leading up to September 1985 (Lind 2002; Jorgensen, Grosh, and Schacter 1992, 3). In 1985, to attend to the crisis, the Bolivian government, headed by Victor Paz Estensoro of the MNR (Movimiento Nacional Revolucionario), implemented a radical, neoliberal restructuring program called the "new economic plan." The new economic plan, introduced by Presidential Decree 21060, was backed by the business sector and disseminated through policies known as structural adjustment programs. The IMF- and World Bank–supported structural adjustment plan sought to "rescue" debtor countries, stabilize the economy, cut inflation, and restore external and internal financial equilibrium and promote growth (Phillips 1998, xv; Jorgensen, Grosh, and Schacter 1992, 3–4). The "rescue" extended by the IMF, however, had strings attached: Bolivia had to relax protectionism and accommodate the needs of the global market.

The first phase of the reforms was to open Bolivia to the international market economy (Álvarez 1996) and suspend state subsidies. The removal of price controls resulted in increases of about 1,000 percent in the price of basic consumer goods (Kohl and Farthing 2006; Painter 1998, 39). Furthermore, opening the country's borders to food imports stepped up competition for agricultural producers (including many producers in Punata and the larger Valle Alto area, causing several to abandon production all together), who were, in turn, unable to compete with the cheaper imported goods flooding store shelves, particularly from Chile and Peru. The fragile textile and food industrial sectors were devastated; more than 120 factories closed. The government also sought to curtail spending by freezing or cutting salaries and laying off ten thousand administrative employees and twenty-five thousand rural teachers (Kohl and Farthing 2006, 71–73). Concurrently, in October 1985 the market for tin (Bolivia's main official export) crashed, which led to the closing of several of the national mines. This resulted in the loss of employment for twenty-three thousand miners, who were granted lands elsewhere in various parts of the country (Healey 1997). Over the course of the year, unemployment rates rose dramatically.

Along with the high unemployment rates, other cutbacks were felt as a decrease in actual wages and represented a "hidden cost" that helped widen the gap between the wealthy and the poor (Kohl and Farthing 2006, 18). For example, many social services (such as health, education, and basic welfare) that had been subsidized by the state were no longer universally available and had to be paid for by individuals (Arze and Kruse 2004; Pereira 1996, 39–40; Toranzo Roca 1997, 199). As well, the tax base changed structurally in ways that negatively affected the poor (Arze and Kruse 2004, 24). Before these reforms, revenue came primarily from taxing income and property; by the end of the 1980s, a shift had occurred whereby more taxes were drawn from purchased products (a system which proportionally disadvantages the working classes). In December 1986 the government created an Emergency Social Fund to alleviate the social costs of the reforms. This fund included resources to be used on small-scale projects that were intended to improve the infrastructure of the country (including street paving and irrigation projects) and to stimulate employment opportunities (Schacter, Grosh, and Jorgensten 1992, 6). In total, 3,045 projects were approved for a total value of 18.1 million U.S. dollars. It was during this period that the GTZ health development project in Punata and the larger Valle Alto area was initiated.

Another phase of the new economic plan was the decentralization of government power through two main laws, the *Ley de Decentralización* and the *Ley de Participación Popular* (Álvarez 1996, 4), and privatization of nationalized companies. The new laws enacted throughout the 1990s massively restructured the Bolivian state, changing the dynamics and organization of political power, the health services, and the educational system, to name a few. The rationale behind decentralization was that it would make local governments more effective and accountable and thus better able to address their constituents' needs. In addition, the decentralization of funds was intended to improve the infrastructure, particularly in more rural areas. From 1993 to 1997, then-president Gonzalo Sánchez de Lozada continued the neoliberal economic agenda, seeking to make the state more efficient, further opening markets to trade, and selling interests in the largest state-owned enterprises (including oil and gas, telecommunications, transportation, and power) through a process known as "capitalization."

Looking back at the first decade of the implementation of the reforms, one positive outcome was the control of hyperinflation through the dollarization of domestic bank accounts (Dunkerley in Kohl and Farthing 2006). This feat is touted as part of the "Bolivian miracle" and by some standards was taken as an indicator of the reform's success (see Jorgensen, Grosh, and Schacter 1992). Inflation rates, albeit only one means to measure "stability," decreased and remained at 11 percent in 1987 (Schacter, Grosh, and Jorgensten 1992), but economic growth did not materialize as expected. In fact, the reforms had profound social costs among the already destitute populations of Bolivia in terms of soaring unemployment rates, loss of social services, decrease in living standards, and growth in income inequality (Antezana 2000, Léons and Sanabria 1997 b). In light of the social costs to the poorest populations, numerous adaptive strategies (some more lucrative than others) served as "safety valves" against the pressures of the reforms. These included increased rural-to-urban migration and a swelling of the informal economy, the coca/cocaine boom of the 1980s and 1990s, and increased international migration.

Patterns of increased migration to areas outside the Valle Alto have a much longer history than the period surrounding the implementation of the new economic plan. Tin miners, for example, regularly traveled to active mines in highland regions throughout the twentieth century. After the 1953 agrarian reform many *campesinos* (peasant farmers) in the Valle Alto received parcels of land that, over time, were further fragmented among subsequent heirs. By the 1960s the demands made for land led many families to migrate to urban areas and the lowlands to secure work in harvesting (Kohl and Farthing 2006, 63). From 1983 to 1985 a severe drought affected many agricultural zones of the Cochabamba Valley and further accentuated the need to migrate in search of employment. During the implementation of the new economic plan, as unemployment rates rose and as borders were opened to cheap imports, the agricultural sector took a further hit. This decline caused an engorgement of the informal economy (including increased street vending by campesinos as well as by former factory workers, miners, and teachers) and the expansion of small-scale economic activities (Buechler, Buechler, and Buechler 1998). By some estimates, by the end of the 1980s and into the 1990s the informal economy expanded to nearly 70 percent of the urban workforce (Arze and Kruse 2004, 28; Kohl and Farthing 2006, 61).

Without access to formal modes of employment and with the intensification of income inequality often associated with neoliberalism, many people weathered hardship by resorting to the coca/cocaine industry. Traditionally, coca and coca chewing has been utilized throughout the Andes in rituals, as medicine, as a way of cementing social relations, as a means to stave off hunger, and as a source of nourishment for thousands of years (Allen 1988; Conzelman et al. 2008). Coca leaves must be processed and significantly altered to produce cocaine, but the two products are often erroneously conflated, and coca production is therefore a polemical political issue internationally. During the 1980s coca production not only met demands of local use but also found a profitable niche in providing the raw material for the international cocaine market. Coca growing absorbed the shock to the unemployed and underemployed including miners, agricultural workers who formerly supplied goods to the mines, and other campesinos who could not compete with prices of imported food goods (Antezana 2000; Léons and Sanabria 1997b). People could be directly employed in the production, growth, transport, and/or stomping of coca, or their relationship to the industry could be more indirect (in roles people were more willing to admit) as people provided services to those directly involved in the trade (see chapter 3). The coca/cocaine economy thus absorbed available labor and also became key to the reproduction of formal economic activity (Toranzo Roca 1997, 195). Indeed, Kohl and Farthing (2006) assert that one reason the new economic plan was able to produce immediate stabilization was because of the dollarization of the economy and decreased regulation that enabled the laundering of cocaine profits without much scrutiny. As will be seen in chapter 3, the lack of regulation enabled the proliferation of risky investments that left many investors vulnerable.

From the mid-1980s until 1997, it is estimated that coca growing and the elaboration of cocaine paste provided between 5 percent and 8 percent of the GDP, exceeding all other agricultural products (Kohl and Farthing 2006, 71). While the boom itself lasted until the end of the 1980s, when overproduction caused a global decrease in the price of cocaine paste, the cost of coca fluctuated throughout the 1990s but remained an important source of income for many. In 1989, President George H. W. Bush initiated a National Drug Control Policy to address the proliferation of drug use in the United States. Central to this strategy was the onset of the "war on drugs," which focused on targeting the supply of production rather than the demand of consumption as key sites of intervention. An important component of Bush's plan was eradication of coca fields and the interdiction of cocaine shipments from Andean countries. Bolivia, Colombia, and Peru were also required to pass a biannual certification process that would grant them "favored nation" status and upon which economic aid was established (CEDOIN, 1991). A positive certification was bestowed on countries meeting the United States' eradication goals. Given the imperialistic overtones of this policy and the ritual role that coca plays for Quechua and Aymara peoples, this plan was met with great resistance by campesinos, whose dissent took the form of roadblocks to major cities and popular protests.

During my extended fieldwork in the late 1990s, Bolivia continued to produce one-third of the world's coca. While production for ritual consumption was legal, the vast illicit production supplying the raw material to cocaine producers supplied jobs to thousands of peasants (Léons and Sanabria 1997a). In 1997 Hugo Banzer (a former military dictator who had ruled in the 1970s), was reelected to the presidency and subsequently implemented a more severe coca eradication program, known as "coca zero." The program had devastating effects on the regional economy as well as across the country (Kohl and Farthing 2009, 63), and numerous human rights violations (including extended incarcerations without trials) took place during the implementation (Conzelman et al. 2008). The Bolivian state compensated coca growers $2,500 for every hectare of coca eradicated. The market price during this time, however, had shot up to roughly $9,600 for the same amount, providing little incentive to cease production (Antezana 2000, 19). Furthermore, the international market for the alternative crops (such as soybeans and oranges) was protected by a very strong lobby in the United States (Léons and Sanabria 1997a, 26), thus it was not as profitable to seek out alternative crops.

The Effects of Neoliberalism on the Ground

During my extended fieldwork, people continuously complained about the stagnant economy. The decline of coca/cocaine paste production affected the economy on several levels. In Punata, the effects rippled throughout different sectors of the formal and informal economy. The incomes of transportation workers, for instance, plummeted. While in previous years, bus, taxi and *truffi* drivers were regularly hired to go to the Chapare region, the crackdown on coca production all but halted travel to the Chapare. As incomes decreased, so did purchasing power, thus affecting many market women and small-business owners. Sarita, a meat vendor, for example, commented, "Before, they used to let us [produce], but now they are very strict. You should have seen Punata ten years ago; it was a different place and people all had money. I used to sell a lot more meat back then, but now there are no sales." Paola, a fruit vendor, similarly remarked, "Sales? There are no sales. The money doesn't flow. Because before, when the people were working in the Chapare with the business of cocaine, the money used to flow then, but now they've put a stop on all that." The effects of the crisis were felt throughout different occupational sectors as well. One dental technician lamented the standstill of business in his office. While only years earlier many people requested cosmetic procedures, these procedures in the late 1990s were not as common. "Before, people would come and request that their teeth be gold-plated [a public demonstration of affluence]," he said. "But now there is no income, and on top of that many people have lost their crops to el Niño."

To confront the challenge of "making ends meet" in a stagnant economy, many families turned to emigration to seek income-generating possibilities abroad. During the late 1990s most of the people I knew had relatives who had migrated to Argentina, the United States, or Israel. For many families, remittances were a principal part of a household's income. It has been estimated that from the 1980s to the late 1990s there were more than 1.5 million Bolivian immigrants in Argentina alone. Concentrated primarily in Buenos Aires, male migrants typically worked in the construction industry or textile factories, and women often found jobs as domestic workers. By the late 1990s, however, Argentina's own economy collapsed when similar economic reforms were implemented there as had been in Bolivia a decade earlier. The ability to regularly send remittances subsided, and many people either returned to Bolivia or migrated elsewhere (Whitesell 2008). When I returned to the field in 2003 and 2006, people no longer spoke as frequently about spouses or siblings in Argentina; rather, most talked about the new exodus to Spain and other countries in Europe.

Throughout the 1990s and early years of the twenty-first century, migration and remittances stimulated the local formal and informal economy in Bolivia. It also fueled a variety of opportunities for potential migrants to be swindled out of their hard-earned or borrowed funds. Numerous travel agencies emerged almost overnight, as did an entire informal set of services offered to those seeking to emigrate. Urban travel agencies throughout the country as well as in smaller towns such as Punata, for example, offered not only services normally expected—such as the sale of flights and booking of hotel rooms in Europe (accommodations many migrants found did not exist when they arrived at their final destinations) but also services tailored to address the needs of individual clients. Among these: teaching people of Quechua and Aymara descent how to "pass" as tourists. This entailed altering or eliminating the material markers of their "indian-ness," class, and gender (Weismantel 2001; Van Vleet 2005). Young women intending to migrate were thus encouraged to shed their pollera and to dress *de vestido*, in Western clothing, and to cut off the long braids that cascaded down their backs. Rural women and men with little experience living in the city were said to be shuttled to the top of an escalator in an upscale shopping mall, where they were taught how to get on and off the contraption gracefully. Rumor went that numerous Bolivians had been deported from Spain because they stumbled on the stairs, drawing attention to themselves. Travel agents, like opportunistic "matchmakers," introduced clients to one another, forming couples who would then travel together to Spain as "honeymooners" in hopes of maximizing their ability to pass the border. Once they did, the "couple" would never have to see each other again. Informally, a number of jobs emerged for "passport processors," savvy men and women who could navigate the bureaucracy of national offices, fill out paperwork, and charge exorbitant prices for those who did not have time to stand in lines or who were intimidated by the process. The wave of immigration to Spain and its ramifications for family relations, health, and well-being will be further explored in chapter 5.

From 1996 to 2010, one of the main preoccupations of my interlocutors was how to endure financial instability. The repercussions of the economic recession (whether from the decrease in coca production, the effects of el Niño, or the effects of the reforms) were commonly reframed into more personal, bodily problems and symptoms. Whether people spoke of *pena* (sorrow), *tirisya* (pining for someone), rage, or envy, or whether they expressed fear about how one could no longer trust one's neighbors or even one's relatives, their narratives became important sites for understanding how people experienced their sense of belongingness (or lack thereof) to the new Bolivia envisioned and promised by national leaders.

The economic and political reforms set in motion during the 1980s also had moral dimensions as they called for a new type of Bolivian citizen—one who could be self-reliant and entrepreneurial, one who could be modern and take advantage of the opportunities that would unfold in Bolivia because it had opened itself to the forces of globalization. Indeed, hegemonic ideas of "progress" percolated through people's intimate wishes and desires (Canessa 2005a; Van Vleet 2005), but the pathways to advancement remained obstructed by hierarchies of race, class, and gender that privileged some citizens over others. Furthermore, the economic reforms and the intensification of income inequalities reconfigured people's self-identities and sociability among neighbors, spouses, parents and children, comadres and compadres. Punateños navigated the social repercussions of neoliberalism with varying degrees of success, drawing upon social and material networks. Indeed, efforts to maintain good social relations was considered central not only to one's ability to make ends meet but, more generally, to good health. To appreciate the articulations between everyday stresses, conflicts, and transgressions—and their relationship to expected "rules of sociality and sociability"—requires a closer look at what social relationships, social hierarchies, and means of cementing sociality were available in Punata. In essence, we must ask what "the social self" (Desjarlais 1992) was like and must examine how people identified, how they related to one another, what tensions emerged between residents, and what expectations they had of one another.

Sociability and the Social Self in Bolivia

Understanding how people link emotions to ill health hinges on awareness of the intricate webs of power relations in the community. People negotiate and perform multiple intersecting identities of race, class, gender, religiosity, relatedness, and seniority, and they interpret their relationships to others through many of these (often essentializing) categories. Building upon the work of Foucault (1978) and Butler (1990), recent scholarship by Andrew Canessa (2005b) and others has called for more nuanced examinations of identity as something that is continuously produced, relational, and performed through social interactions and exchanges (Weismantel 2005, 181). From this perspective, social interactions between husbands and wives, parents and children, neighbors and comadres, market women and their clients, or doctors and their patients are all fertile sites where identity unfolds. In Punata, people self-identified in numerous ways, depending on where they were, whom they interacted with, and what aspects of their identity they wished to highlight in a given situation. Furthermore, emotional expression, constructs, and embodiment are phenomena that are tightly bound to the contours and structures of age, gender, class, and ethnicity. Such insights are pivotal to understanding the links between emotion, sociality, and health.

While individuals have the agency to perform their identities, they do so from within the "parameters" of local scripts, meanings, and discourses that shaped their understanding of the world around them. As Van Vleet (2005, 108) insightfully points out, "Gendered, racial, cultural and linguistic relationships of power shape an individual's capacity to act" and hence his or her ability to perform or challenge a particular identity. Punateños and Punateñas thus draw upon numerous hegemonic racial, ethnic, and gendered discourses that contrast groups against one another, assume hierarchies, and shape interactions between them. For example, many people envision the town of Punata as being composed of a small number of more prosperous elite who see themselves as "superior" to the middle- and working-class populations. This class structure does not neatly graft onto ethnic or racialized categories, although the elite are more likely to be perceived as *mestizo* (having Spanish heritage), while the middle- and working-class are seen as having "more" Quechua ancestry. Social interactions between these different groups are crisscrossed by numerous ethnic, linguistic, age, religious, and gender hierarchies. In Punata, people also often identified as *vecinos* (neighbors); *gente bién* or *gente decente* (good or decent people) to make distinctions between themselves; town-dwellers; poorer *campesinos* (peasants living in more rural surroundings); *gente de las Alturas* (people from the highlands); and *forasteros* (strangers or foreigners) (see also de la Cadena, 1996). Vecinos could include mestizos/mestizas as well as people who would identify as *cholo/chola*. *Chola*, an ethnic term used for a woman who is considered "part" Indian and "part" mestizo, was a category marked by the fact that these women wear the traditional pollera (de la Cadena, 1995; Weismantel, 2001). They are often also called *cholitas*. A woman who does not wear the pollera was called *de vestido* (of [Western] dress).³ *Cholos*, the male counterpart, were not marked in the same way by their clothing but were often marked by their wearing of *abarcas* (sandals whose soles were made from recycled tires) and were more likely to be seen as darker skinned and less educated than those who identified as mestizo (Canessa 2012; Van Vleet 2005). Campesinos, also referred to as *laris* or more derogatorily as *indios*, were considered indigenous Quechua and largely illiterate; most *indias* also wore the pollera (see Weismantel 2001 for an examination of racial categories in the Andes).⁴ *Vecinos*, in general, were considered more prosperous than the subservient and less-educated campesinos, who regularly experienced discrimination.

The boundaries between ethnicity and class were continuously shifting and somewhat blurred in these categorizations. The terms used are dynamic, fluid, and relational in nature so that while, in Punata, someone who lives in town could refer to someone as a campesino, from the perspective of the city of Cochabamba most Punateños themselves would be seen as campesinos. As well, a person could play upon others' ethnic perception of them to maximize their advantages in a social interaction (de la Cadena 1995; Paulson 1996; Seligmann 1989). Discrimination among vecinos and campesinos was also based on distinctions of gender, class, ethnicity, and age. Subordination thus could have many different faces and could have occurred in varying degrees (Ehlers 1991; Weismantel 2001). Among intimates, gender subordination did not just flow from men to women but also from women to women, particularly when these women belonged to different class, ethnic, or age groups, or according to their position in familial hierarchies (Van Vleet 2002).[5] The way people interacted had acute ramifications with regard to emotions and their management. This will be further explored in chapter 2.

Power relations within households and among different members of the family are shaped by gender and age hierarchies. In the case of many women, these traditional hierarchies were often "upset" or contested. Sometimes women headed the household because husbands had migrated; other times women were the main or sole income earners or had unemployed or underemployed spouses, which caused marital tensions. Children (including grandchildren) of different ages were relied upon for an array of responsibilities: childcare, cooking, running errands, watering fields, watching storefronts, and so on. They were also expected to be good students. Indeed, investing in their children's education was one of the main ways that market and other working women spent any surplus earnings in hope of providing at least some of their children the possibility of a "profession" outside of market vending (Seligmann 1989). Female family members usually shouldered household chores (particularly if mothers spent their day vending in the market), although in some households boys were also taught to cook and launder clothes. Extended families regularly helped each other as well: during harvest time, by sending food to one another, or by helping with childcare. Older children (most often girls) might be expected to work to help send a younger sibling to school, a practice that sometimes caused conflict in families. Marta, for instance, a thirty-year-old market vendor, was often resentful that her mother had selected her (as the oldest child) to work in their market stall so that together they could earn enough income to send the youngest siblings to college. Marta attended school until the fifth grade and then began working full time. She became pregnant out of wedlock at age eighteen and then also had to earn money to support her son.

Like Marta, many of the market women I knew lived with their partners for several years before marrying at the courthouse or at a church. The initial years of marriage could be difficult as couples struggled to set up their households or acquire independence from their parents. For some, the first years of marriage could also be marred by domestic violence (Larme 1998, Van Vleet 2008) and infidelity. Many women regularly accused husbands of having affairs, and this often became the source of much tension between couples, particularly if a wife believed that her husband's lover was resorting to sorcery as a way to make the man "wander" or become abusive toward his wife and family. Often, prevailing notions of machismo exonerated men from fault. Furthermore, in a context of regional and international migration, it was often assumed that when a man ceased sending remittances, it was because he had set up another household (see Boehm 2012 for the case of Mexico). Some couples, if able, migrated together but often had to leave young children under the care of grandparents.

Numerous studies in the Andes have examined the importance of another source of social support and sociality: *compadrazgo* (ritual kinship) ties and reciprocity (see Albro 2008; Lagos 1994; Van Vleet 2008). Ritual kin ties help establish a relationship of reciprocity and exchange between people considered to be from different social hierarchies, or to solidify an affective tie that may already exist between individuals. There are numerous occasions during which these relationships may be forged: baptisms, first communions, graduations, patron saints' days, fiesta days, and weddings, to name a few. As people come together in celebration of particular life-cycle events, ritual kin ties can also help abate the costs of such festivities (Albro 2008). During a wedding, for instance, numerous ties can be established, and the highest honor (and responsibility) is bestowed on the *madrina/padrino de matrimonio* (godmother/godfather sponsoring the couple). They will be looked upon for advice and support throughout a couple's married life. These godparents often purchase the wedding rings. Other people will be asked to sponsor other parts of the wedding, such as invitations, party favors, the band, or the cake, among other things.

Compadrazgo is an important way to extend one's social network in a community and in the workplace. Among market women it was a very important way to cement relationships between one another. Compadrazgo ties change the way two people interact and what they can expect from one another. The relationship of compadrazgo, however, is not always "utilitarian" or forged with only economic gains in mind. Having a particular comadre or compadre in town can often also be a source of pride or a sign of affection.

As mentioned in the introduction, the chichería in Punata and throughout the Cochabamba valley plays a vital role in Punateño/a sociability. Its place in society and history, and its role in the local economy, has been explored by several social scientists (Classen 1993; Rodríguez and Solares 1990). People meet at chicherías to socialize, do business, hold meetings, celebrate, mourn, or just drink together. Financial or political agreements are often cemented over a glass or gourd of chicha, and the beverage plays a prominent role in everyday religious fiestas, birthday celebrations, funerals, and carnival activities. The etiquette of chicha drinking has the tendency to encourage excessive consumption. Chicha is most often drunk in a group with others, but no chicha may reach one's lips without first and foremost making an offering to the *Pachamama* (the early mother) in the form of a *ch'alla* (an offering in which a small amount of chicha is poured on the ground). Drinkers take turns "inviting" each other gourds or glassfuls of the beverage. The process of reciprocity in Andean rituals and quotidian events has been examined extensively in the literature (Allen 1988; Classen 1993; Rasnake 1988; Weismantel 1988). The same set of expectations surround chicha. While "taking breaks" between drinking rounds is acceptable, to turn down a serving repeatedly, and particularly from a single individual, can be taken as a personal affront. While I conducted an interview in the market, Doña Eulalia, a coca seller, came to offer us some chicha she and her husband had made. We initially politely turned it down so we could proceed with the interview. We continued with the interview for another hour; Doña Eulalia returned to offer us chicha again. She left behind two full glasses and returned fifteen minutes later to pick up what she expected would be empty vessels. When she noted we had not yet consumed the drink she angrily protested: "What is the matter? Why are you not drinking? Do you think this is poison? I myself made

Figure 2. Chicheria

this chicha, I know it is pure [not tainted or poisoned]." We apologized and readily drank what was before us. Many women complained they often did not feel like drinking but did so to avoid conflicts with the person making the offering.

People socialized around chicha, and the chichería was one of the main places where men and women often felt they could express their emotions and forget their problems for a while. Sitting before her daughter's storefront one evening, Flora told me: "When you have problems or sorrows [penas] you go to the chichería to forget your sorrows and your problems for a little while; you drink some gourds and you forget. But the next day, its worse," she continued, laughing. "Besides the sorrows you also have a headache!" Her husband Juan added, "One goes to extinguish [apagar] one's sorrows, you go there and you forget your disappointments; to laugh a little with your compadres and to forget your daily problems." His daughter, who disapproved of his drinking, chimed in: "One never forgets! People go because of vice; its a bad habit and that's why they go!" Others similarly reflected on why people drank:

> They go because they have a vice, because it doesn't do anything to them [doesn't make them sick], and each time they come back. I guess they forget a little bit of their worries and sorrows; they talk among themselves, they tell one another what is happening in their lives; and sometimes they fight or cry as well. Other times they sing and laugh. But actually, the way I see it, it's just a plain vice.
>
> They come and drink, argue, they cry or they just hang around alone and quiet. Then once drunk they are able to express and say things that normally might be difficult when sober.

Many women had ambivalent feelings about the consumption of chicha. "In moderation," drinking chicha could be a pleasurable and uniting experience. All too often, however, women felt that people drank excessively (and they readily admitted to doing so as well), and this could often lead to violence in the home. Many women complained about the drinking that takes place during Tuesday's feria (the day of the regional market) because much of the profit that can be made on that day is spent on consuming chicha. A repeated scene I witnessed in Punata on the afternoon of the feria was that of angry women literally dragging their husbands or sons out of chicherías, yelling at them for spending their hard-earned money. Apart from the negative aspects of heavy drinking, the chichería from a local perspective provided people with a significant social space where emotions could be expressed and shared.

Furthermore, it allowed people to avoid the accumulation of emotions that can potentially lead to illness.

The general insecurity many Punateños/Punateñas felt in the wake of the neoliberal policies was also further reflected in the skepticism toward the state. In the widespread restructuring of the economy numerous social services were curtailed or sacrificed, leaving the state unable to fulfill its obligations to its citizens. Such was the case concerning the provision of police and judicial services. During a time that unemployment rates were rising and the gap between rich and poor was widening, national police budgets were being cut. One result of this was a fourfold increase in crime rates across the country from 1993 to 1999 (Goldstein 2005, 399). While people in Punata were well aware of rising crime rates in urban centers and accepted that violence was a part of everyday life in the metropolis, they also were concerned about the increase in crime closer to their doorsteps. This significantly increased people's sense of vulnerability, insecurity, and helplessness. Numerous scholars have addressed the increased skepticism that the working classes in Bolivia had toward the police and toward the legal system (Goldstein 2003, 2004, 2005; Vilas 2008). This pessimism was widely shared in Punata, where many people felt crime would be left unaddressed. Everyone knew that in order to get something done by the police, a bribe or intimate relationship to someone in the judicial system was necessary. While laws, regulations, and sanctions did indeed exist, they were not democratically or effectively applied to all citizens: race, gender, ethnicity, and class shape the rights ascribed to different individuals. Some citizens were, thus, more citizens than others (see Canessa 2005a, 3).

* * *

In this chapter I have sought to sketch a broader picture of the political, economic, and social landscapes against which different emotions and experiences of illness unfolded and which will be explored in subsequent chapters. Neoliberalism is a broad term that has numerous tenets but also multiple manifestations in different contexts. The context of Bolivia is a particularly interesting one, as the economic reforms unfolded concurrently with a coca boom that, in many ways, helped mitigate the negative effects of the reforms. An examination of sociability and social relations in the context of Punata followed from this larger, national context.

In their day-to-day interactions people invest politically, morally, and emotionally in their social relations: with immediate family, ritual kin, neighbors, or co-workers. It is through these investments that market and working-class women construct networks of economic and emotional support. But sometimes investments go wrong, and relationships fail or people disappoint: husbands batter, daughters get pregnant before finishing their studies, neighbors or even family members become envious, co-workers backstab, sons are unable to enter the workforce. Furthermore, while the underprivileged might view those faring well as "selfish" and those who are also struggling as "uncooperative," those who are comparatively wealthier in terms of actual or social capital often feel overwhelmed by the expectations family and community members might have of them. Comadres and compadres who may have served as mutual pillars of support can grow distant as the children of one couple succeed professionally while the children of the other drop out of school. Successful market women may interpret their failing health in terms of the envy of their co-vendors; a woman raising her children alone while her husband works abroad may unexpectedly learn that his failure to send remittances is due to his infidelity rather than his inability to find work. Young daughters-in-law who aspire to progress economically through migration may be pejoratively labeled "ambitious" and ungrateful for rejecting alternative opportunities extended by their mother-in-law. These and numerous other sources of conflict wear away at social ties and what people believe they can count on. As Das and Kleinman (2000) aptly point out, "[When] faith in trusted categories disappears, there is a feeling of extreme contingency and vulnerability in carrying out everyday activities" (8). When people claim "*las cosas ya no son cómo antes*"—"things are no longer the way they used to be"—they are often referring to how social interactions have changed in their own lifetimes and how this causes uncertainty and unease for them. Rules of sociality and the underlying expectation that interactions between community members will be reciprocal are challenged by the national discourses of modernization and progress as well as an individual's drive, ambition, and aspirations (Van Vleet 2008, 48).

These failings of sociality must be read among a confluence of factors that extend beyond just one individual disappointing another. Relationships and expectations among Punateñas unfold amid the challenges posed by economic uncertainty and increased migratory flows that leave many households fragmented, racist legacies that limit people's ability to enter the workforce, and conflicting ethics that privilege individual ambition and progress over mutual aid and reciprocity. In chapter 2 I will further examine sociality and interactions between neighbors and kin as they relate to the expression of emotions and the emotional "privileges" granted to some during social interactions.

2

Physicality's Sociality and Sociality's Physicality

Fluid Boundaries of the Body

Father Cresencio was known in the community as a rather stern, middle-aged priest who seldom missed an opportunity to tell his parishioners they could do better: they could collaborate more with one another, they could spend less money on sponsoring fiestas, they could come to church more often, and they could be mindful of the suffering of others. "¡*Nos riñe siempre!*" laughed several women from the market: "He scolds us all the time!" In spite of this, people often found solace in talking with him; as such, my conversations with him sought to explore what role he played in helping people resolve their everyday emotional, health, and economic crises. Although Father Cresencio initially denied that parishioners came to him for health problems, during one interview he further reflected upon my questions and reconsidered:

> There are many people who come to penance who don't begin their confessions with a list of their sins; rather they start with [a list of their bodily ills]: "my head hurts" or "my stomach hurts" or "I don't feel well these days." They relate their physical ailments with psychological and spiritual ones, . . . Or in confession they tell me "I think I am ensorcelled and that is why I am suffering from this illness." My role is to give them advice and peace. . . . Often people want to do the same [to others as is done to them]; they want to avenge an act of sorcery with another. I tell them not to return evil with evil. I tell them to believe in our almighty God and to increase their faith.

In the context of Punata it makes perfect sense to start a confession with a list of bodily complaints and ailments. A person familiar with the local theories of illnesses and symptoms readily knows about the intricate interrelationship between emotions, symptoms, and sociality (Tapias 2006a, 2006b; see also Finkler 1994 for the case of Mexico; Scheper-Hughes 1992a for the case of Brazil; Tousignant 1984 for Ecuador). As David Orr argues, in many indigenous cultures "illness is less the isolated manifestation of pathological symptoms within an individual than it is a disturbance in the social relationships of which the sufferer forms part" (2013, 695). Thus, to begin a confession with a list of debilitating ailments positions the teller as a victim—a sufferer—and leaves open the ambiguous possibility that an unjust, unfair offense has taken place. The list initially signals the consequences of emotional turmoil and concern about one's social relationships. As the confession unfolds, however, the elaboration of the parishioner's bodily symptoms foreshadows what will likely shortly follow: the admission of the sins the teller may have committed against his or her families, neighbors, co-workers, or the community at large. The symptoms can be the result of an individual's own emotional upsets (the accumulation or "mismanagement" of one's own emotions), or they can also signal the emotional upset of others who in turn have channeled their fury through sorcery (*hechizo*) to harm the teller: in both cases the underlying common denominator is a failing of sociality.

In times of economic hardship the social transgression committed can include any number of acts: selfishness and the inability to reciprocate favors; failure to pay back loans or to extend a loan to someone in need; lying; stealing; tipping the scales in the market in order to maximize profits; engaging in violence toward one's wife or children; or simply wishing someone ill fortune. Confession offers parishioners a time to reflect on how their actions and behaviors may have incited other's envy and recourse to sorcery and allows the teller to repent without necessarily having to confront those he or she may have wronged.

Father Cresencio's narrative also provides interesting insights into local worldviews and conceptualizations of Andean bodies that place emphasis on relatedness and the fluid boundaries between physicality and sociality. Numerous scholars working in the Andes have examined the intimate physical connections between living bodies and between bodies and the natural and spiritual worlds (see Allen 1982, 192; Bastien 1987; Canessa 2012). The individual and social bodies are intrinsically interconnected throughout the Andes: action in one physical or emotional sphere can exert effects in another. The boundaries of the body as I understood them were deeply challenged in the context of Punata but provided me with a better understanding of how illness processes were conceptualized and lived. At the beginning of my fieldwork, when people told me that their illnesses were related to sorrow, rage, desire, pining, or any number of other emotions, what I was failing to grasp was an understanding of the body that was profoundly intersubjective and the degree to which conflictive social relations or hardship could themselves be embodied.

Emotions and Corporeality in Punata

During my extended fieldwork, people spoke of emotions such as rage and sorrow (two of the emotions most commonly linked to ill health) as if they were "fluids" or substances that accumulated in the body or were transformed into other harmful substances. Rebhun briefly mentions that the women she worked with in Brazil viewed emotions as "energy" that acted according to the "same physical properties as water" (Rebhun 1994, 366; 1999). In Punata, both the etiological explanations for how emotions made people sick and the treatments people administered attested to this physicality. For instance, emotions were said to accumulate in the body when not expressed, and this posed noxious effects to the body. If people did not find a means to express their emotions, these could also be transformed into other pernicious substances that then had to be eliminated from the body to avoid illness. Such views of emotions as "fluids" are part of a larger hydraulic view of the body wherein equilibrium not only of "hot" and "cold" qualities (referring not always to temperature but also to a general quality of foods, illnesses, and medicines) but also of the flow of substances and fluids are central to the maintenance of good health (Bastien 1987; Classen 1993; Hammer 1997).

Emotions, however, were understood not to be internal only to an individual such that they would affect only those who "felt" things such as sorrow, anger, or envy. Rather, emotions could also circulate or be "passed" on to others. Specifically, a mother could transmit her sorrow or rage to her child through her breast milk or through the placenta; envy that one individual felt could have physical effects on others through the effects of sorcery. This transmission of emotions fits nicely into a larger belief system concerning the body, corporeality, and sociality among Andeans. Recent cross-cultural scholarship on kinship and the circulation of children, for example, has brought to light the multiple ways in which "relatedness" is constructed across cultures (Carsten 2000; Franklin and McKinnon 2001; Leinaweaver 2008). Among many Andeans, relatedness does not solely rest on consanguinity and affinity but is something that must be continuously produced and reproduced through feeding, through sharing substances, and through the care and nurturing of others (Orr 2013; Walmsley 2008; Weismantel 1995). Weismantel, for example, working in Ecuador, examines how the feeding of a child and the circulation of products of the same hearth are what constitute the basis for relatedness. As one materially feeds a child with the products from one's fields (which themselves are nurtured through the labor of the family), the bond between the child and his or her caretakers is materially made. The child ingests what his or her "kin" ingest, and through this process these bodies become linked through shared substances. Thus, Weismantel concludes: "Those who eat together in the same household share the same flesh in a quite literal sense: they are made of the same stuff" (1995, 695). Krista Van Vleet (2008), also investigating relatedness among a Quechua community in Potosí, Bolivia, examines how relatedness is grounded in ideas about *ayni* (reciprocal exchange relations) that are built and solidified through continuous social, emotional, and material work (77). Similarly, in Punata, the belief that emotions have physical attributes and that they can circulate between different bodies speaks to these more general notions of embodiment and further melt the boundaries between bodies and their physical and social milieus. The emotions engendered through social and power relationships can be circulated, transmitted, and shared with other bodies. The remainder of this chapter explores *how* women conceptualize emotions and the ways emotions can harm the body and then turns to an examination of *what* these views of emotions and the body do for the maintenance of particular hierarchical social roles.

The Accumulation of Emotions

On any given day in the market, one can invariably see women wearing tiny coca leaves or the halves of a fava bean on their temples. These small objects, carefully positioned, are said to be "sucking out" rage or sorrow that has accumulated in a person's head. The leaves or beans, it is claimed, alleviate some of the minor symptoms such as headaches or dizziness that can emerge as a result of an upset or sorrow. The "sucking out" of emotions is a common therapeutic practice in Punata. Women concurred that it was not only feeling emotions that automatically rendered them sick or unable to work; the ability to express and "discharge" their emotions, and thus prevent their accumulation, was critical in determining whether or not they became ill. Lutz describes a similar finding among residents of a Micronesian atoll in which emotions must "come out" in order to alleviate the trouble they can cause (Lutz 1988, 100).

For the most part, the head and stomachaches stemming from quotidian preoccupations, frustration, anger, or sorrow did not interfere with daily responsibilities and hence did not warrant being called "illnesses." More serious ailments such as *embolio* or *aire* (terms interchangeably used for what biomedicine terms "stroke," usually accompanied by a partial paralysis and loss of speech), however, were attributed to the excessive accumulation of emotions. In everyday life one was continuously releasing emotions over time, but each individual body had a "limit" to the amount that could be endured. Once these limits were surpassed, the potential for illness increased. The slow accumulation of emotions could be variable, occurring over the course of a day, months, or even years. At the least expected moment, even a minor altercation could serve as the catalyst for symptoms, as illustrated in the following comments:

> Sometimes it's not necessary that you have strong rage. Sometimes, without even noticing it, you get angry, and in that case you get sick. For example, you get angry—but you didn't really even notice that you got angry—but sure enough, shortly after, your stomach starts to hurt. In this case it was already accumulated. . . . When one goes getting angry, getting angry, it accumulates, and then when someone throws one little insignificant offensive comment your way, it's enough [to make you sick].
>
> I get angry, get angry, get angry [*reniego, reniego, reniego*], and it accumulates in me. It accumulates, accumulates, I get angry, I get angry and it accumulates and that's it, that *embolio* wants to get me [*ese embolio me quiere dar*].

The accumulation of emotions such as rage and sorrow could be avoided or alleviated through crying, expressing the emotions or being distracted from them, or by drinking, as numerous women's comments reflect:

> We hold it in, see? That's why we get embolio. But when one cries until one gets tired, then that's the end of the problem. When one cries, there is nothing left, everything is released. But if one doesn't cry, the attack can come. That's where the embolio comes from; if you cry, nothing happens.
>
> Sometimes when I get angry I am capable of killing someone, but just at that moment. . . . It is only that instant though that I am really angry—I'm like a match. And then it goes away. "Flora, don't get angry," [the other market women] tell me. "Don't get so furious," [and then] they make me laugh and it goes away. That is good, they tell me; that way the rage does not accumulate.
>
> Sometimes out of sheer sorrow I go to drink chicha. I know its bad for me but then once I throw up I feel better. I get rid of all that sorrow and only then do I feel better. Its almost like a tranquilizer or an injection. If I don't throw up I'm all agitated, but if I throw up I am tranquil.

The daily disappointments layered over other ongoing problems can lead to the accumulation of emotions and distress. What upset individual women and what caused them to fall ill was contingent upon their long, personal trajectories of suffering and the ways they were able to negotiate their emotions in the face of social interactions.

Transformed and Eliminated Emotions

If emotions were not expressed, there were other vectors through which they could "come out" and thus not accumulate in the body. One vector was through vomiting, as the above description demonstrates; another was through their transformation into other substances, such as bile. In addition, rage, sorrow, fright, or desire could be eliminated through breast milk or through the uterus. If elimination occurred through breast milk or through the uterus, the emotions were not so much transformed as they were "passed on" to the body of the breastfeeding or gestating infant.

Many people asserted that when they felt great rage it was transformed into bile. A person then would either vomit the yellow/green substance voluntarily or physically induce vomiting. Excessive drinking can also encourage the elimination of bile through vomiting (and hence could have positive effects):

> The rage that I hold in, all that gathers, I throw it up, and only after that I feel more calm and tranquil. That yellow and green stuff, all that I throw up. If I don't vomit, I remain the same, all upset but when I throw that up I feel better.
>
> When you feel rage, little by little it accumulates, your gall bladder gets loaded. If it's loaded I start feeling sick, I get dizzy, nauseous, and then I throw up the bile. . . . Once the bile comes out, little by little I start to feel better. I must expel bile about every two months; several times a year. The last time it happened was Monday morning.
>
> When you get really angry it becomes bile and that is what is harmful. We have to throw that up; if not, it can kill us. It's very bitter when we throw it up, and in that stuff comes out all our rage. At least that is the way I am; when I get angry, I am not tranquil until I throw up all that bile.

As reported, if the bile was not expelled, it accumulated in the gall bladder, and, in severe cases, the organ had to be removed through surgery. If surgery was not possible, then the excessive accumulation could kill. Many people spoke of the production of bile as a positive protective mechanism of the body. When someone talked about vomiting bile, that itself was not considered an illness or a symptom of ill health; rather, it became an important means through which someone could *avoid* more serious (and incapacitating) illness.

Another important vector through which harmful emotions were eliminated from a woman's body, particularly if she was not in a position to express them or orchestrate them in a way that dissipated their negative effects, was through breast milk. In such cases, the woman herself did not become sick because her infant ingested the emotions. This often caused a series of infant illnesses, the most important of which was *arrebato*, an ailment further explored in chapter 3. Any emotion a woman felt, such as anger, sorrow, cravings or desire, fright, preoccupation, or frustration, could pass to her child through her milk. Thus, prior to feeding, many women regularly expressed the first few drops of their breast milk and discarded it—particularly after any sort of social altercation or conflict. The egregious emotions could also be drawn out of an infant with herbal baths. Indeed, a common folk therapy was to bathe the infant's legs with a concoction of coffee and other herbs. Women would also pass "positive" emotions such as happiness, tenderness, and joy, which contributed to an infant's overall well-being.

During pregnancy a mother's emotions could pass to her infant through her uterus and, in extreme cases, could cause miscarriage. Fetuses were said to be particularly vulnerable to the emotions a mother felt because they were still developing and their bodies were not yet strong. The effects of strained sociality could thus begin in the womb. Punateñas were particularly careful not to upset, anger, or sadden gestating women, lest they be held responsible for a miscarriage or a breastfeeding child's illness. A mother's food cravings were also said to pass to infants and negatively affect them. Thus, a pregnant woman was continuously offered food (whether she wished to consume it or not) and was considered "irresponsible" if she turned down the food offered:

> If a woman is pregnant and she "desires" but has no money to buy what she craves, then she can easily have a miscarriage [*aborto le da*]. When a woman is pregnant, she can really desire everything! So people see you pregnant and they immediately offer food, even if they don't know you. . . . Some pregnant women say, "Don't worry, I don't have cravings." But we say, "You might not crave, but your baby does," and so she has to accept. We always give them whatever we have. . . . If she doesn't accept, she can either have a miscarriage or the baby is born and can't close his or her mouth and drools all the time. And when people see that, people yell at the mother, "*Bandida!* You craved and did not eat! You should have eaten!"

If the mother was seen as the vector for the negative effects of cravings on a child in utero, she was equally seen as the vector for treatment. The mother had to eat the desired food and, in the process, she would pass the food to her child through her uterus, and the child's cravings would also be satisfied.

However, since mothers also did not know what a baby might crave in utero, it was expected that they would accept everything that they saw others eating.

The Politics of Emotional Expression

The "mechanics" of the accumulation and elimination of emotions provides insights into how the body is seen to function. However, such mechanics are also tightly interlaced with subtle structures of gender, class, ethnicity, and age; that is, these views of emotions and their relationship to well-being *do something* socially: they help keep particular age, gendered, class, and ethnic hierarchies in place. For many women, the ability or failure to maintain health—their own and their infants'—was linked to numerous social constraints and women's ability to navigate the power relations in which their lives were embedded (see also Rebhun 1993). In the case of rage and sorrow, women's ability to orchestrate their emotions (by expressing them or not) was directly linked to negotiating the intricate webs of power relations (between genders, ethnic groups, classes, and ages) and assessing the possible risks that could result from such expressions (Abu-Lughod and Lutz 1990).

Across cultures, emotional expression and suppression are social practices that men and women engage in and are central to the way they respectively perform gendered and other identities. In Punata, *where* a conflict takes place, *with whom*, and over *what* shapes how a person expresses and addresses emotions. The expression of emotions was not always possible or favorable, particularly in public places where people worried that others would see and criticize them (Clark 1989, 113; Dunk 1989; Glass-Coffin 1992; Krieger 1989). Thus the articulation of different facets of one's identity to the context of a particular conflict or crisis ultimately rendered "emotional privileges" to certain members of the population while denying them to others. Abu-Lughod and Lutz aptly assert that expression hinges on "power relations that determine what can, cannot or must be said about self and emotions, what is taken to be true or false about them and what only some individuals can say about them" (Abu-Lughod and Lutz 1990, 14). Thus, when a particular social context proved inappropriate for expression, a person might "hold in" their emotions, an act perceived as harmful to the body but one that simultaneously kept particular hierarchies and privileges in place.

In social interactions of numerous kinds, it was a plain and simple fact that some people had more liberty to have emotional outbursts than others or were seen as more emotional than others. These interactions were shaped by hierarchies of age, gender, and class. The elderly in Punata, for example, were the recipients of much social respect and attention. People showed much concern for the well-being of elders or those who live alone because their children have moved to other places. It is not uncommon for people to affectionately refer to the elderly as *abuelita* or *abuelito* (grandmother or grandfather) even if they do not share a kin tie. Schoolchildren regularly spent Sunday visiting their grandparents or elders. Given the lack of extensive social services for the elderly in Bolivia, the primary responsibility for them lay with the family, who regularly made gifts of food and attended to their needs.

In light of the social respect bestowed on the elderly, when market women had conflicts with someone older than themselves, they seldom argued back. Women complained of daily, mostly insignificant arguments with customers, but if these occurred with an elder, they would rarely engage in the argument. "You can't argue back, you just have to stay quiet. You have to respect your elders." Another woman who owned a little convenience store said, "Well I can't argue with them, I can't just yell at them as I do my kids, I just have to hold it in. But then once I'm alone, if they really upset me, then I get it off my chest [*me desahogo*] and I cry. Out of respect for the older person. If they insist that they want something I tell them calmly I don't have it and never raise my voice." Most people thought it wasn't worth the energy or the social criticism that such an argument might engender and would usually just listen patiently to the elderly customer's complaints. Children, in contrast, often received the brunt of people's frustration or anger.

Gender also profoundly influenced the expression of emotions. For instance, how women and men reacted emotionally was intimately tied to the ways they performed their gendered roles. Gender scholars readily acknowledge that both femininities and masculinities are not homogeneous categories but rather are unstable, flexible, and continuously reenacted through social interactions with other men, women, partners, kin, and community (Boehm 2004; Pribilsky 2004, 2007; see also Guttmann 1996, 1997). Indeed, Inhorn and Wentzell, focusing on masculinity (but equally applicable to notions of femininity), argue that gendered identities are "ever in progress" as individuals' behavior shifts, depending on whom they interact with, when, and in what contexts. While there is not a single "model" that encapsulates the multiple forms of femininity and masculinity that take shape in Bolivia, when it comes to emotional expression, the stereotype evoked was that women are more emotional than men (see also Lutz 1990) and hence have to orchestrate their emotions frequently and carefully. By extension, women were also seen as more likely to experience illness or symptoms (see Larme 1998). Indeed, the stereotype of the "macho" male included such attributes as being "strong," being one who did not "cry" or express emotions (lest his masculinity be threatened), being a "provider," working hard, and acting as an authority within the household (see Gutmann and Viveros 2004 for a discussion of masculinities in Latin America).

In Punata, women generally understood their greater "emotionality" (in contrast to men) to be related to the fact that they shoulder more of the daily hardships of life. Women often claimed their husbands did not worry, feel sorrow, or experience sadness in the same ways as they did, saying that, in fact, the way men dealt with these emotions was by causing more sorrow and suffering to those around them. A closer analysis of the naturalizing of gendered emotionality, however, reveals that an emphasis on women's greater emotionality assists in the obfuscation of the many ways masculinities were threatened, reconfigured, and redefined throughout this period of economic and political history. Among many couples, power relations shifted or were strained as men had to take on new roles in the household division of labor. Furthermore, male unemployment, out-migration that left women as heads of households, and increasing pressure on women to meet domestic expenditures realigned patriarchal norms in households. Many men experienced uncertainty and dis(ease) about masculinity, self-reliance, and autonomy, and individual men reacted differently to such challenges: at times they reconfigured their views of masculinity, but at others they actively sought ways to further entrench such views.

Many of the market women I interviewed were the sole or main income earners in their households. The hardships they experienced emerged from balancing what Moser (1993) has called the triple roles that women are expected to engage in socially: reproductive work (childbearing and childraising responsibilities), productive work in income-generating activities, and community-managing work. For some women—as "single parents" who were either abandoned by their husbands or were married to men who had migrated abroad to find employment—these roles were even more taxing. Under the stress of such responsibilities, women generally concurred that they were more likely to feel particular emotions and hence would have to express or "control" them more often than men.

On many occasions both men and women would find solace from their sorrows, rage, and preoccupations in the chichería. Chicherías were places where people socialized, drank reciprocally, rested after a long day's work, celebrated special occasions, or drowned sorrows. A common refrain repeated in Punata was "When there are sorrows, you should lean on the *pendón*." The pendón was a six-meter-tall flagpole often posted outside a chichería, indicating that chicha was available. Drinking chicha to the point of inebriation, while often a source of distress between couples and in families, can also be a time of great joy, merrymaking, and sharing among friends, family, and the community at large, both for men and women. People would often say that chicha gave people courage to say things that ordinarily might be difficult to say. A young man, for instance, might drink to build up the courage to ask a girl out or express their feelings for her. Women might openly express dissatisfaction about a class conflict. I noticed that when I first arrived in Punata, it was under the influence of alcohol that men and women usually told me their saddest stories, sorrows, or preoccupations. They related stories of unmarried daughters that they were worried about, about health problems, fears of sorcery, or a conflict with neighbors. I was very often moved by their stories but quickly learned the etiquettes of these moments. Frequently by the next day I was told that they had been "outside of him/herself" (*fuera de sí*) and couldn't remember a thing about the previous night, perhaps in embarrassment or over regret for having expressed vulnerability.

Numerous scholars have addressed the role alcohol consumption plays in social and ritual life in the Andes and the wider Latin American area (Allen 1988; Gutmann 1996; Lancaster 1992; Rasnake 1988). Several of these scholars have been rightly criticized for their essentialized statements on men and alcohol consumption, statements that obscure the fact that many men do not drink or get violent when they do drink. In Punata, a man who drinks a couple of times a week is not overly criticized publicly, particularly if he does not become violent.[1] In contrast, if a woman were to go to a chichería regularly (and particularly if she went alone), she might be seen as irresponsible and her behavior marked as shameful. Furthermore, what happens *after* drinking is what is seen as having negative effects on women. Among the women I interviewed it was the exception rather than the rule to meet a woman who had not experienced some form of domestic violence linked to drinking (either from a husband, father, or other relative). Fear over the physical battering they might receive made many women cautious in expressing their emotions during a conflict with their inebriated husbands. Furthermore, as women aged, their grown children were protective of them, and mothers often feared fights between sons and fathers.

Class and ethnic differences also often framed the type of expression that could ideally ensue between people. This was particularly visible in places of employment where employees were expected to respect their bosses or supervisors and often "swallow" their feelings of anger or frustration. The fear of losing employment (which was not readily available) often made people tolerate abusive situations and mistreatment. Class differences were also visible in the ways market women treated their numerous clients. With money at stake, people were continuously negotiating for better prices, products, and services. One woman's comments reflect the deferential treatment she gave to her wealthier clients compared with how she treated peasants who might come to purchase from her stall:

> When I get upset [at a client] I have to put up with it [*tengo que aguantar*]. If someone says something that upsets me, I have to hold it in or else the others [other vendors] would look at me poorly. But not with the elderly; you have to treat them with respect. Or with the *gente decente* [the decent people], you know, the people from the pueblo, the people with resources [*la gente de tener*]—you have to look and judge who you are dealing with. With the people from the *campo* [peasants] you can't lower yourself to their level. If it's gente decente you must argue respectfully and with manners.... When a señora [a lady] comes and starts complaining about my prices or my products, I kindly tell her "No Señora, it is not that way." But UY! sometimes these señoras also treat us badly. Here each day we get aggravated by the clients.

Indeed, the biggest arguments I witnessed were between market women and poorer clients. But the quote above hints at why this was so. Market women had little to lose by arguing with peasants. An argument with a wealthier client, however, might mean losing that customer permanently. On the other hand, peasants were often trying to maximize their purchasing power. One agricultural worker who regularly came to the Punata market said, "[Market women] make you feel like you are worth nothing. They think that because you are poor they can treat you however they wish!"

The negotiation of emotional expression was a daily undertaking wherein the costs and benefits of expression were carefully evaluated. In this process people found ways to discharge their emotions by confronting offenders or remaining silent. If the latter option was chosen, women found other means to discharge their emotions: with other clients, with co-workers, with their children. Or, in a worst-case scenario, they would just swallow their anger and risk the harmful accumulation of emotions.

Natural Environment and Time

Punateñas were readily able to voice the idealized social prescriptions and proscriptions for the expression of emotions. These ideals were not always met, and, in fact, it was the disruptions of such ideals that often led to conflicts (a finding echoed by Clark 1989; Dunk 1989; Krieger 1989; Van Schaik 1989). But in addition to considering the context of a social encounter and the ways emotions could or should be expressed, there were unintended and uncertain ways in which emotional expression could prove harmful in relation to the natural environment, again pointing to the interrelatedness of all living things. There were particular times of the day and places in the Andean landscape that were considered treacherous with respect to the expression of emotions. Illnesses like Pachamama (a term for an ailment whose symptoms can include hives and swelling, and a term that refers to Mother Earth) and susto were said to develop at *saqra hora*, the Devil's hour, which comes around several times a day, although there was considerable disagreement among my interlocutors regarding the exact hours of danger, and some adamantly reported that there was no way of knowing. "If we knew when these *saqra horas* happen, we wouldn't walk around during these times to avoid the risk." Others were certain that the hours were close to sunrise (around 6:00 A.M.), noon, and at sunset (approximately 6:00 P.M.), while others questioned whether these hours really existed at all, arguing that the risk was omnipresent.

Not only was the time of day when emotions were felt important, but where emotions were experienced mattered as well. There were places in the landscape where illnesses were more likely to manifest themselves (Larme 1998). These include rage, sorrow, or fright for the case of Pachamama or fright for the case of susto. There were a number of places scattered in the landscape that were treacherous, referred to as *lugares virgenes*, "virgin places," or the areas over old, dried-up water holes or wells. In these places, the Pachamama (Earth Mother) was said to be hungry and could take away the person's health if he or she experienced rage or sorrow there. Many people also said that the Pachamama was angered by the expression of these emotions in these places. The assorted pains and symptoms associated with the illness Pachamama were said to flare up during the saqra horas, although some patients claimed that their symptoms were continuous.

The dialectic relationship between physicality and sociality in Punata is essential to understanding health and illness in Bolivia. Andean notions of corporeality and emotionality hinge on the flow of substance (food, emotions, substances) within bodies, from one body to another, and between bodies and the natural environment. As emotional expression is a pivotal way to understand the relationship among emotions and illness and symptoms, it is also important to consider what these views of emotions impart socially in helping to maintain particular types of social interactions and hierarchies. As such, in the following three chapters the inextricable link between the social and the physical are examined as we explore the illness experiences of several women and children.

3

The Intergenerational Embodiment of Social Suffering

On a brisk Tuesday afternoon in June 2003 I headed over to Sabrina's house, which was located two blocks from Punata's main plaza. I had met her through my field assistant a week earlier, and she had invited me to visit her at home so we could chat *más tranquilas*, in a more relaxed way and without interruptions. I had passed her house many times on my way home from the market but didn't know she lived there. The paint on the mustard-yellow adobe house was chipping off, and the heavy wooden front door was left ajar, as was common in Punata. I knocked loudly, holding my breath as I waited to see if one, or more, barking dogs would come to scandalously announce my arrival. Relieved that none came, I relaxed and waited.

When Sabrina opened the door, she seemed surprised to see me and had probably forgotten our appointment. She quickly wiped her wet hands on her apron, reached out to hold mine and exclaimed, "*¡Que bien que has venido!*" "How great that you came!" Sabrina was dressed in blue jeans and a grey sweater. She invited me to sit down around a shaky wooden table in the front room of her house. As I sat, she swiftly moved into the next room and mumbled something to someone I could not see. A moment later, a little boy with a mop of black hair, rushed past me in his flip flops, smiled, and headed out the door as his mother called out: "*¡Apura, Papito!*" "Hurry up, love." We sat together at the table in a room typical of many Punata households: the walls were peach colored; in addition to the table there were six chairs, a small altar in the corner of the room decorated with flowers and candles, and several outdated calendars of scantily clad models on the wall. Above the door hung a small bunch of dried yellow retama branches, intended to ward off ill wishes and envy. In no time, the little boy (who I would later learn was Sabrina's son) returned with a glass liter-bottle of Coca-Cola, excited that—thanks to the visitor—he would be able to enjoy some. Sabrina headed back to the kitchen and a few moments later returned with a full glass in one hand and a big plastic bowl of pea pods in the other.

While she shelled peas at a pace my fingers would never be able to match, we talked for several minutes about our respective families and eventually got around to the topic of motherhood, which was what I had originally planned to interview her about. As the twenty-nine-year-old mother of two boys, ages eight and eleven, and a two-year-old girl, Sabrina had plenty to say about the topic. She responded to my questions quickly and confidently, talking enthusiastically about the qualities of a good mother.

> What's a good mother? Well, you have to take care of the baby very well, provide for it. You should talk to the child, make them understand things. . . . You should not be too volatile; you should do your best to avoid sorrows. I, for instance, would try not to feel sad or angry about things, all with the purpose of not making my daughter sick.

However, upon hearing her own words, Sabrina paused (as did the crisp "clicking" of the pea pods), frowned, and said: "Actually, no one can be a good mother because there is always someone to make you angry."

Like most women in Punata, Sabrina had a clear sense of what entailed "good" mothering. While "getting angry" or frustrated at the mischief of children may be seen as an expected part of parenthood across the world, there is more at stake in Sabrina's statement than first meets the ear. For pregnant women and women with young infants, in particular, one important definition of a good mother was a woman's ability to "control" her emotions so as not to harm her breastfeeding or gestating infant. In a context of economic uncertainty, drought, poverty, and domestic violence, however, such control was often difficult to exercise. Insufficient money to pay for rent and food, unemployed husbands who squandered money, children who desired new clothing or toys they saw on TV (which were often beyond the reach of a family's income), the daily vigilance of neighbors (*miramiento*), and the ill wishes of those who were envious—all these things could unleash feelings of frustration and despair.

The economic precariousness many women faced was the cause of significant distress among mothers, which in turn caused short- and long-term health effects in their infants and children. Although many studies have focused on the effects that poverty and social change have had directly on children (Pribilsky 2001; Scheper-Hughes 1992a), my focus is on how market and working-class women in Bolivia perceived children's health to be affected *through* mothers' faulty emotional responses to distress and through their bodies. Women's bodies were thus seen as the potential vector for both transient and enduring ailments and debility in their children. The cases presented are read within a confluence of circumstances that provided fertile ground for the proliferation of distress among many Punateña women. The government's implementation of radical economic reforms encouraged free enterprise and less regulation; the principles of neoliberalism exacerbated already existing social hierarchies, and Bolivia was enmeshed in the global "war on drugs," which, at the time, was atrophying a related informal economy (and engorging others) that helped sustain many families.

Both men and women in Punata often spoke about how "money didn't run" (*no corre plata*), implying that no one had money to purchase goods and services. This had not always been the case, but economic conditions had gotten more difficult in the late 1990s, and many families struggled to make ends meet. People viewed politicians as continuously making promises (but failing) to improve the economic conditions of Bolivia. The economy remained weak, with one important exception—coca growing. As discussed in chapter 1, Bolivia is one of the top three producers of coca leaves, the raw product for the production of cocaine. Parallel to this production, however, were active national and international efforts to eradicate coca, which simultaneously suffocated the secondary economy that flourished around coca growing. These eradication programs, largely sponsored by the United States, formed the cornerstone of the war against drugs (Garcia Argañarás 1997; Sanabria 1993; Spedding 1989).

Since the mid-1970s the local economy in Punata became increasingly tied to the nearby coca-growing Chapare region, situated just a mountain range away. Although a region of much sociopolitical conflict, the Chapare was the place to which many people from Punata migrated in search of supplemental income. Even if people were not necessarily directly involved in growing coca themselves, they could find gainful employment in an array of activities that formed part of the informal economy that sustained the area. For example, many women I knew migrated seasonally to sell lemonade, *mocochinchi* (a drink made from dehydrated peaches), or set up food stalls in the region. Men who ordinarily drove taxis in Punata or Cochabamba realized they could make greater profits by shuttling people back and forth from the Chapare or by transporting coca leaves or kerosene (needed for the elaboration of cocaine paste) from fields to stomping camps. While conducting my extended fieldwork, there was increased international pressure to curtail coca growing, which, in turn, curbed the extensive traveling that occurred between the Valle Alto and the Chapare, further restricting household incomes.

The narratives that follow in this chapter trace the experience of two working-class women, but their stories are in many ways representative of those evoked by other women. My focus on the intricacies of these women's experiences enables me to examine the entanglement of the interrelational politics of emotional expression, gender relations, and the effects of the economic reforms and the coca industry at a local level. The economic and social precariousness under which these women lived reshaped gender and familial relations and intensified their suffering and the suffering of their children. The first story analyzes the experience of a woman named Elisa, an impoverished peasant who was regularly battered by her unemployed husband, Juan. The second story is that of a woman named Rosalía, a hospital janitor, who lost her life savings in a banking scam. The suffering of both women, although clearly experienced at the individual level, was also seen to pass to their infants through their bodies. Elisa saw her distress as being passed on to her infant through her breast milk, resulting in a syndrome locally known as *arrebato*. Rosalía's distress, in contrast, affected her infant in utero, which had long-lasting, negative effects on the health of her son, who was nine years old at the time of our encounter.

The analysis of these cases provides insights into how people live in their bodies and experience the changing world around them, how they exercise agency in difficult circumstances, and how this is related to the emergence of emotion-related illnesses. How emotions were conceptualized and how emotional expression and power relations figured into the narratives of their everyday interactions with others are vividly demonstrated in the stories told by Elisa and Rosalía. But a full understanding of these cases also requires an appreciation for how breastfed infants and those developing in the uterus were seen as particularly vulnerable to the emotions of their mothers. Finally, each narrative is linked to larger economic issues that negatively affected the health of women and children throughout the 1990s.

Maternal Emotions, Breastfeeding, and Infant Illness

Although much has been written about women's bodies and health, less attention has been paid to in-depth, qualitative examinations of breastfeeding (Blum 1993; Kaufman, Deenadayalan, and Karpati 2010; Maher 1992;

Scheper-Hughes 1985; Tapias 2006a; for reviews of the literature see Dettwyler and Fishman 1992; Van Esterick 2002). Zietlyn and Rowshan (1997) argue that while breastfeeding is a universal behavior, until fairly recently scholars have tended to overlook the way cultural and social forces shape the practice.[1] When examining breastfeeding practices in Bolivia, how a mother's emotions may influence the quality of a woman's breast milk and the way gendered politics intertwines with talk about breastfeeding bodies is where the researcher's focus should necessarily be.

As described in chapter 2, accumulated emotions have the potential to render a woman sick, particularly if she is not in a position to express her feelings or orchestrate them in a way that dissipates their negative effects. However, if a woman is breastfeeding, the vulnerability then shifts to her infant: a woman's accumulated emotions could pass through the breast milk and cause harm to the nursing child. Flora, describing how her infant son had once gotten very sick from her rage, explained: "If a mother gives her breast to her child when she is angry, the child can die because all that rage she is passing in her breast. She does not get sick, doesn't feel indisposed, [but] she transmits everything. The baby sucks out all that rage." Among most infants, this ingested rage would manifest itself in the form of *arrebato*. This ailment, the symptoms of which include stomachaches, incessant crying, severe diarrhea, and vomiting, was related to a mother's inability to shelter her child from the accumulation of her rage or sorrow. In extreme cases, arrebato could be fatal. In fact, along with susto (fright illness), arrebato was cited by women in Punata as one of the main causes of infant death. However, if treated in a timely manner, arrebato could also be cured. Thus, in some cases the effects of the mother's emotions passing to her infant were short lived and treatable; but in other instances a mother's milk could be seen as permanently affected and inadequate for consumption. Women in this latter category were said to have milk that was *leche gatona*.

A mother could transmit "poisonous" or tainted breast milk to her infant particularly when she was under social and/or economic distress (see Farmer 1988; Mull 1992). Domestic violence, economic hardship, social conflicts, and mistreatment were experiences that could affect the physical and nutritional qualities of a mother's milk. However, in most cases, once the mother returned to a state of emotional tranquility, the milk was said to return to normal as well (unlike leche gatona, which was seen always to be inadequate). Thus, it was not only "negative" emotions such as rage and sorrow that affected the child; the child's well-being also hinged on what might be considered more "positive" emotions, such as happiness and tranquility, which are similarly transmitted through breast milk.

When a woman was known to have an unusually difficult home life and/or to suffer from economic constraints that led to constant sorrow and preoccupation, her milk was more likely to be seen as leche gatona and thus permanently affected and damaged. Such women were actively discouraged by family members and friends from breastfeeding their children, leaving infants potentially vulnerable to other health hazards, as the local water was unsafe for consumption. When recommendations to cease breastfeeding were not followed, mothers were seen as irresponsible and carelessly endangering their infants.

Some, but not all, women embraced the view of their milk's poor quality, particularly after experiencing the death of an infant or a child affected with arrebato. Leche gatona was seen as physically different than healthy milk, of poor quality and harmful to the child. It was described as: "watery," "transparent," "loose," "not thick," "weak," "lacking nutrients," "phlegmy," and bordering on having a bluish tint to it (see Mull 1992; Scheper-Hughes 1985). Inherent in these descriptions, however, were also moral and emotional commentaries on whose body the milk came from and the position of said body vis-à-vis other bodies. In this process, gender and class hierarchies were maintained, reinforced, or challenged. Mothers would rarely openly describe their own milk as having poor qualities; rather, these assertions were often made by others and became a judgment about the bodies, class, and ethnicity of those with less power, such as peasants, poor women, or employees. Marta, whose mother owned a restaurant in the central market, for instance, discouraged her maid from breastfeeding her newborn child:

> That maid of mine, Teresa—her milk is not thick, it's blue, very watery. Of course people from the *campo* [countryside] [like Teresa] don't eat anything nutritious, they can't afford it. Teresa used to make her children sick all the time. She would breastfeed her little girl and the child would start crying. I used to say to her "don't give her your breast! Your milk is no good! Why do you give her your milk if it does not satisfy her?!" She used to have an abundance of milk but it was blue, it was just no good. I made her stop breastfeeding at three months. My milk, on the other hand was very thick and abundant, and my baby was very fat while he breastfed. Even the doctor told me my milk was good.

The views of the maid's milk exemplify what Oths (1999) and Miles (1998) see as tendencies of the dominant classes in the Andes to define the peasant body as coarse and vulgar—and, I would add, weak and deficient. These views were further complicated by Marta's own aspirations to prosper and distinguish herself from other workers in the market. Marta's parents did not give her the opportunity to attend college because her labor in the family restaurant ensured her younger siblings could attend college in Cochabamba. Marta was quick to medicalize the quality of her maid's milk, attributing the problem to malnutrition. In framing Teresa's inability to feed herself and care for her body as the cause of her weakened milk, Marta sought to deflect blame from her own contributions to Teresa's distress as her employer. Marta was heavily in debt and paid Teresa poorly; Teresa, in turn, was unable to provide adequately for her two children. Although Teresa had "an abundance of milk," she was ultimately persuaded to believe that her milk was inadequate, and so she quit breastfeeding at three months.[2]

The discourses on when and when not to breastfeed had varied effects on mothers themselves. Some did not accept that their milk was bad. Juana, who was told she had leche gatona after her first infant died, contested this view by retrospectively examining her experiences: "I confirmed this wasn't that way. People told me that my milk was no good, that I was too *renegona* [volatile], and so when I had [my] second [child] I decided not to breastfeed, but that one died as well. It had nothing to do with my milk. It was God's will [*la voluntad de Dios*].

A faithful Jehovah's Witness, Juana saw the death of her first child not as proof of her poor milk, but rather, as part of God's larger plans. Juana did manage successfully to breastfeed her next three children. Some women with leche gatona, however, do decide to stop breastfeeding. Laura, age thirty-five, decided to cease breastfeeding her two children at three months and two weeks, respectively:

> My milk was no good, it wasn't thick. I used all kinds of home remedies to try to increase my milk . . . but they didn't work. I had "leche gatona" which is a watery milk which looks phlegmy, and that is no good for the baby. People would tell me, "You are going to kill your baby with arrebato." The things you get angry about pass onto the baby, and I've always been *cascarabias*, irritable, so I decided to stop giving her my milk.

By bottle feeding, Laura was able to deflect blame and remove the burden of responsibility for her child's potential illnesses from herself and what she saw as her volatility.[3] While Laura embraced the view that her milk was "no good" and that her body and "character" were faulty, her choices were also influenced by middle-class aspirations to be a professional woman. Formula feeding helped re-legitimate her as a caring mother and also facilitated her return to work as a dental assistant. As part of a dual-income household, Laura also had the economic means to purchase formula for her infant, an expense that many households were unable to shoulder.

Other women who continued to breastfeed while accepting that their milk caused their infant's illness often deflected fault from themselves and placed it on the person who caused conflict, such as a husband, child, neighbor, or stranger. Flora believed this as well: "The person who made the mother feel angry, that's whose fault it is. The person who makes a breastfeeding mother angry should know better." Laura echoed this comment when she said, "People are not conscious of trying not to make you angry. They treat you the same way. They don't value the state you are in [as a breastfeeding woman]." Some women, however, such as Sonia, accepted that it was their responsibility not to have emotional outbursts: "It is the responsibility of the woman . . . of the mother . . . not to feel anger or feel sorrow because the others are just going to treat you the same way. They have no consideration for you." In expressing such beliefs Sonia became an active reproducer of particular gender roles and views of how women should deal with their emotions. While frustrated that people did not grant special treatment to women who breastfed, she was willing to shoulder the responsibility for "controlling" her own emotions. Discourses of blame, however, were contextual; many times mothers blamed themselves (as was the case with Costa, who told me, "I killed one of my babies with that arrebato") or were blamed by others for causing the child's illness ("The mother is too bellicose, she needs to control herself more!").

Finally, it is important to note that many women often evoked the threat or actual diagnosis of arrebato in an effort to solicit social support and make distress publicly known to others (Rebhun 1993). Vera, in the midst of a heated argument with her jealous husband, "threatened" to breastfeed her infant: "We'll see what people will say when this baby falls ill." She was certain people would side with her and blame the infant's illness on her husband's excessive suspicion of her. Upon hearing her threat, Vera's husband backed down.

Regardless of whether a woman believed she had leche gatona or not, mothers were always attentive to the effect their own emotions could have on their breastfeeding babies. As such, mothers often took great care after a conflict to rehabilitate and restore the quality of their milk. Mariana, owner of a small shop, explained:

> When a woman feels rage and she has to breastfeed . . . let me explain it this way: I got angry and [then] have to give my son my breast. Before I give him my breast I have to discard the first few drops of milk. That milk is not like normal milk, it is blue-ish. You let that milk fall to the ground or just discard it. That milk looks like serum [*suero*] except it's sort of blue, sort of purple. I

think it must have some chemical. If you removed a certain quantity of milk from your breast, then little by little the milk color returns to normal. It is only then that you can give your baby your milk. You can give your milk only after you have removed the contaminated milk.

Although women took care to express and discard tainted milk, many believed this preventive practice was not always reliable. A child could still develop illness in spite of the preventive practices exercised by his or her mother. Such was the case of Elisa's child who developed arrebato and whose story I relate below.

Elisa and the Predicaments of Expression

Elisa was a twenty-six-year-old cholita who lived with her husband, Juan, on a small plot of land where they grew carrots and carnations to sell in the local market. The couple and their infant child lived in a one-room adobe house with no electricity on the outskirts of Punata. They had not always been as economically strapped as they were at the time of my fieldwork, but over the years they had become increasingly impoverished. Their small carrot farm was not very profitable, and a past drought had negatively affected their crops. A few years earlier, Juan had been a taxicab driver and made regular trips to the Chapare, taking Punateños back and forth and occasionally transporting coca leaves. But the crackdown on coca growing meant there was a lot more risk involved in working in the Chapare, and fewer people, including Juan, were taking up jobs there. For example, along the main highways to the Chapare there were regular checkpoints through which cars had to pass in order to be inspected for transporting restricted materials (such as coca and kerosene); fines were doled out when drivers could not present the necessary permits to haul these materials. As efforts to eradicate coca intensified in the late 1990s, imprisonments related to repeated offenses grew exponentially, as did human rights violations (Conzelman et al. 2008; Garcia Argañarás 1997). For many, including Juan, the personal risks involved in working in the transportation industry were not worth taking. However, with the income generated from these trips gone, Juan could no longer meet the transportation union dues he was required to pay in order to drive his car as a taxi. At the time of my interview with Elisa, Juan had been unemployed for several months, and his frustration was often directed toward his wife. His loss of employment in many ways threatened not only his sense of masculinity and of being a "provider" but also shifted the power dynamics in the household (Inhorn and Wentzell 2011). The financial dependency strained his relationship with his wife on multiple levels.

According to Elisa, in efforts to raise some money to invest in the farm, Juan decided to sell his fifteen-year-old car. Mariano, a neighbor, expressed interest in purchasing the car and paid them a $300 down payment, promising subsequent monthly payments for the total agreed upon. Although Mariano was not an experienced driver, Juan and Elisa agreed to the sale, and considering he was a *conocido* (someone known to them, not a stranger), they let him take the car. The car's papers would be transferred to Mariano's name when payments were complete. Mariano was late in subsequent payments and skillfully avoided Juan and Elisa for several weeks. When Juan and Elisa caught on, Juan managed to confront Mariano in an effort to recover his car. During a heated discussion at a local chichería, Juan found out that Mariano had an accident that had caused significant damage to the front of the vehicle. Enraged, Juan came home intoxicated that evening. He took out his anger on his wife and beat her severely during an argument.

This was one instance, among many, of the battering that Elisa regularly experienced at the hands of her husband.[4] When I visited her house the day after this incident, her left eye and upper lip were swollen. In a calm and unaffected voice Elisa explained she had not wanted to argue with her husband, as he was "outside himself" (Harvey 1991). In fact, Elisa was repeatedly treated at the local healthcare post for injuries related to domestic violence. Elisa went on to say that on other occasions, when Juan was not drunk, she would likely have argued back. Many other women I interviewed who found themselves in disputes with their intoxicated husbands made similar assertions.

Elisa explained that a few hours after her husband hit her, she carefully removed the first drops of milk from her breast, discarding it on the pounded dirt floor in an effort to remove the tainted milk from her breasts. Shortly after, she proceeded to feed her son. Within hours, the infant's nails, mouth, and feet became purple, accompanied by severe diarrhea. To Elisa, her child became sick with arrebato because she had been unable to express her emotions and confront Juan, fearing this would further enrage him. Even though she had taken care to remove the first drops of her breast milk, this had not been enough. The emotions had passed into her breast milk and the baby had sucked out her rage and sorrow and had thus become sick himself. The child's health condition, however, slowly improved over the course of the day.

At the local level, the degree to which arrebato was a threat to Elisa and her infant was directly related to her social position, how she dealt with her emotions, and the self-monitoring processes that she enacted to protect her child's health. The links between larger economic and political processes and people's experiences on the ground are not always so easy to trace. Juan's monthly income, which he generated through trips to the Chapare, had been significantly curtailed during efforts to eradicate coca during the international war on drugs. Furthermore, as a person unemployed in what was a very stagnant economy, whose hard labor on the farm did not translate into a sustainable income, and who was apprehensive about the possible additional loss of payments for his car, Juan physically took out his distress on his wife. Elisa, in turn, experienced the violence in very localized and complex ways. How Elisa cared for her own body and the health of her infant presented her with difficult predicaments as she made continuous decisions about her safety and the safety of her child.

Women interviewed consistently agreed that if a woman were unable to express her emotions (orally through confrontation or physically by removing tainted breast milk) but nonetheless breastfed her infant, she herself was less likely to get sick from emotions precisely because her infant would suck and draw them out of her. Although women knew that expressing their rage or sorrow could prevent arrebato, in certain contexts a woman might refrain from such expression if it entailed the possible loss of her job, fueled an argument with her husband, or resulted in tensions with fellow community members. Social roles and statuses were reinforced through the expression of emotions, and women attempted to carefully balance the double-edged sword of expression. On the one hand, if they expressed their emotions, they ran the risk of being criticized or harmed by those who could wield power over them; on the other hand, if they did not express their emotions, they could potentially endanger their infant's health.

Elisa, for example, refrained from confronting her husband (and thus expressing her rage) because she feared further battering. The containment of this rage, however, affected her breast milk. Within minutes of the onset of her child's arrebato, Elisa bathed her infant in herbs that were intended to draw out the rage from his small body. The treatment succeeded and the child recuperated completely. A mother whose child developed a grave case of arrebato was often blamed for the child's ailment by family or community members for her inability to "control" her emotions. Elisa was able to avoid the blame that accompanied arrebato, and her mothering skills were never in question. Although the child fell ill, Elisa had taken the necessary precautions to shelter him from harm. She tried to remove the tainted milk from her breasts; when this failed, she treated the child with herbal remedies.

The negative effects of maternal emotions on infants were not always as temporary as they were in the case of Elisa's child. Sometimes, the consequences could lay latent and have effects later in the child's life. Such was the case when a mother experienced distress during pregnancy.

Maternal Emotions, Pregnancy, and Illness Susceptibility in Infants

Emotions during pregnancy could have numerous health effects on mothers and their unborn children. A mother's distress and emotions could reach her child through the placenta, causing a delayed but generalized debility among children and rendering them continuously susceptible to illness throughout their lives. This susceptibility was referred to as *debilidad*.[5] Debility was always counterbalanced by another conceptual framework referred to as *fuerza* (strength) and helped describe the constitution of a person and/or his or her history of distress and illness.

The tropes of debilidad and fuerza permeated many social spheres. Debilidad not only referred to someone's constitution or state of health, but one could also describe land as being *débil*, infertile and unable to bear good fruits; or the economy or a nation could be *débil*—too dependent on foreign aid, unable to compete or stand up to the demands made by the world market. One could also speak of moral debilidad or fuerza, particularly with regard to sexuality and will power, or to a *carácter débil o fuerte* regarding different types of personalities that explain some life trajectories.

With regard to health, debilidad and fuerza, in Punata, were states or conditions that underlay the health-illness continuum. Debilidad predisposed certain individuals to illness often related to emotions, or it could be a condition that resulted from ongoing illness and suffering (see also Larme 1998; Miles 2003). This relationship was not unidirectional; rather, there was a circularity of influence between the two. "One never heals the same, one is always left more débil" was a repeated comment made by women and men in Punata. These two conceptual categories were not in an "either-or" binary relationship to one another. That is, a person was neither débil nor fuerte but could have different degrees of these qualities in different contextual moments. A person might be sick, for instance, and thus be in a potential state of debilidad, but if he or she was able to carry on with normal activities, then he or she was fuerte in the ability to endure the illness.

Debilidad also helped Punateñas explain why certain people were more vulnerable to illness than others. Certain illnesses were often thought of as animate: that is, the illness was seen as having a will and agency of its own. These illnesses perambulated around the environment, sometimes lurking behind closed doors or around corners, awaiting the right moment and host (see Cartwright 2007 for similar findings in Mexico). Such illnesses had the best chance of flourishing in the person with debilidad, the person with a history of illness or the person least able to manage his or her emotions. A personal history or intimate knowledge of anger, sorrow, and preoccupation could make people more vulnerable to illness and thus experience increased debilidad. One meat vendor in the market voiced this succinctly:

> There isn't just one type of sorrow. You feel sorrow over everything. Right now, I'm not selling meat and I have sorrow over the meat. If I don't sell, with what money will I be able to purchase more cattle? There is sorrow over everything Maria... here in Bolivia, everything is *pena, pena, pena*, sorrow, sorrow, sorrow. Your husband doesn't work, you have sorrow, your income alone doesn't stretch to buy all you need, you have sorrow. You can't buy for your children: sorrow. The husband doesn't have sorrow over anything, if he doesn't work, he simply doesn't buy anything for the children. He doesn't feel the sorrow that I feel. I don't sleep from wondering, "From where I am going to get money? Who will I turn to? What am I going to do?" You suffer, you suffer over everything. Now, if your husband works and you are just a housewife, why would you suffer? In that case, the husband is the one who suffers. He knows what is missing. We feel sorrow because of a lack of money and slow business.

Although adults can develop debilidad at any time over the life course, in this chapter I explore the case of children left with a "constitutional" debilidad resulting from exposure to their mother's emotions while in the womb. Gestating babies have porous bodies that are particularly vulnerable to the suffering of their mothers. The case of a nine-year-old boy named Fernando illustrates this point and also links debilidad to economic factors that affected people across classes in the area of Cochabamba.

Rosalía's Sorrow and Fernando's Debilidad

Rosalía was a jovial, thirty-three-year-old bilingual Spanish- and Quechua-speaking hospital janitor. She was married and had two children: Marcela, age twelve, and Fernando, age nine. Overall, Marcela was a healthy child, but Fernando had been prone to illness since he was a baby. Rosalía described her son as someone who had debilidad—a child who was very nervous, irascible, short tempered, and susceptible to illness:

> This son of mine, he is a very nervous and irritable child. He gets sick easily from rage, and when he gets angry, he turns purple. When he was just a baby and cried, he would turn all purple—his whole body and his mouth, for instance, went from red to purple. And he went growing up that way; he

is very affectionate, but when he gets angry? God spare us! He is unbearable, sometimes his nose even bleeds from the rage that he feels.

Rosalía had a clear sense of how her son developed debilidad. In her lifetime, Rosalía had suffered great emotional turmoil due to a history of domestic violence, poverty, and the loss of her savings in a 1991 bank scam. The combination of these factors, occurring at a crucial point in her life cycle, contributed to what Rosalía viewed as her son's debilidad. A closer examination of these events contribute to our understanding of how local and global factors influence how people subjectively experience illnesses in Bolivia and the conceptualizations of the body that they hold.

Rosalía had married at age nineteen because she became pregnant. The first decade of her thirteen-year marriage was filled with infidelity, as well as verbal and physical abuse. She regularly dreamed of migrating to Argentina (to join many of her siblings) but could not fathom leaving her children behind. She had few kind words to say about her husband, but she did not plan to leave him either.

> I turned twenty in my husband's power.... We used to live like a cat and dog. Why? Mostly [we fought] over money. If the money didn't last, we fought. If I needed to buy bread, we would fight. If there were no vegetables, we would fight. He used to beat me when he had other women.... The life of a man is like that, but I reached my limit. I told him that I would have him notified for pensions [file for divorce], and since then, he doesn't treat me as badly. We always fight but not like before. He used to leave me with black eyes. He would give me a black eye on one side and as soon as it was healing, he would give me a black eye on the other side. He used to go out drinking with women and wasn't with me. He'd go pick up his salary and it all went to pay his debt for the drinking. "Rosalía, I paid the chichería" he would tell me. He gave me all kinds of excuses, he'd arrive here with no money.... He didn't care if there was nothing to eat in my house. I used to go to my uncle's house to eat, that was my main preoccupation—How was I going to feed my children? So we would go there and eat and we would then come home.... He [on the other hand would spend money and] go out to eat. He only returned home to burp! That's what he used to do to us! Life is very tremendous [¡La vida es bien tremenda]!

In the last few years, the violence in their relationship subsided. Nonetheless, Rosalía resented him: "Sometimes I remember the things he has put me through, things you would not believe if I told you, and I just can't find kindness to be nice to him." Rosalía's attitude toward their relationship also changed since she had begun working at the hospital. Workshops on domestic violence and familial life were regularly offered at the hospital, and she used to eavesdrop on the talks while cleaning. Over time, she was able to earn her husband's respect, and whenever he became jealous she would ignore him.

In addition to the domestic strife that had characterized a greater part of her marriage, Rosalía's life had been marked by poverty. Rosalía had gone to school until age fifteen. She then worked for an uncle at a gym; he gave her room and board and a little bit of spending money for her labor. At age nineteen she found a job as a domestic worker and held numerous jobs over the next fifteen years. At her latest job in the hospital Rosalía earned 520 bolivianos per month, which in the late 1990s was worth approximately $90. She claimed she never got sick while working independently, but since working in the hospital she suffered continuously from headaches. Mistreatment and arguments with the doctors and nurses on staff were a regular part of her daily interactions.

Although Rosalía had worked menial jobs for a greater part of her life, and money was a continuous source of contention between her and her husband, she always tried to save whatever she could. For several years she had knit sweaters for a local cooperative, enabling her to earn extra income (see Buechler, Buechler, and Buechler 1998 on the multiple jobs women engage in to maximize income). In the late 1980s, at the encouragement of a friend, Rosalía decided to place her small savings into a local *inmobiliaria*. Inmobiliarias were essentially "building societies" that accepted small-scale investments from thousands of people offering annual interests of 60 percent to 70 percent, as opposed to the 14 percent rates offered at private banks (CEDOIN 1990). As the unequal opportunities of neoliberalism constrained people's ability to make ends meet, the social milieu was rife with people looking for an easy way to make money without any sacrifice or suffering (Nelson 2009). Indeed, many people in Punata had been pressured by relatives, friends, and neighbors to take advantage of the investment opportunity offered by inmobiliarias and coaxed not to be left behind by prosperity (Comaroff and Comaroff 1999).

The economic reforms of the 1980s and the free market they fostered reduced the presence and intervention of the state in businesses. Furthermore, the state encouraged people to *salir adelante*, to "get ahead" and take responsibility for their financial well-being. This new economic context, coupled with a majority population facing scarcity, provided a fertile ground for the proliferation of these savings societies throughout Bolivia, and particularly in Cochabamba. My acquaintances and friends in Cochabamba recalled the investment opportunities as a "craze" that took hold of the population, and where the opportunities and advantages of investment were framed as "too good to pass up." This craze dovetailed nicely with state discourses asserting that *all* could prosper and benefit from Bolivia's insertion in the global economy.

The inmobiliarias were, of course, too good to be true. They were said to be places where profits from the cocaine industry were laundered. Relocated miners, ex-cocaleros (compensated in dollars for eradicating their coca fields), teachers, market women, professionals, students, and even wealthier investors flocked to the inmobiliarias in hopes of maximizing their savings. Expatriates from abroad (in Argentina and the United States) also sent money to Bolivia to invest. Others enthusiastically sold their homes to invest the capital (CEDOIN 1991, 36). In essence, these building societies were acting as saving institutions: unofficial, nonregulated banks that served a dual role. They laundered cocaine profits and also made everyday life more bearable for the unemployed, who could invest their meager savings and live off interest payments. The inmobiliarias, with their timely payment of interest each month, in many ways filled the lacunae left by the state and helped remediate many of the social costs of the reforms, particularly for the poorer populations (CEDOIN 1991, 9).

Many people in Punata, including Rosalía, eagerly deposited their money in these banks in efforts to maximize their earnings and sustain their hopes for a better future. What people did not know was that the hearty "interest" earned by the end of the month was the very money they had deposited earlier. Contributing to a classic Ponzi scheme, investors were thus literally depleting their own savings (CEDOIN 1991, 37). Millions of dollars were embezzled by the directors of these inmobiliarias, leaving thousands of investors out in the cold. Because these societies were to a certain degree illegal (or at least they weren't made to comply with any regular banking laws), the state offered no protection to investors.

One of the most famous and publicized cases of failed inmobiliarias was the case of FINSA.[6] Many people in Punata had at one point invested their savings into this firm—or at least when I asked about the scheme, everyone seemed to know someone who had been swindled. Few, however, were willing to admit they had been duped. One woman, skeptical of the whole "opportunity," phrased it as follows:

> How are they going to give you such high interests for nothing? *No pues.* No way. But everyone became crazy. And it wasn't just the poor people, it was

gente bien that put their money in there: doctors, dentists, teachers. All in hopes for a better life, all wanting to make money. But there is nothing free in life. They lost their houses, they lost their money, they lost everything.

FINSA was established by two brothers from the city of Oruro, Nelson and Eddy Arévalo Páez, who started their firm by opening up a radio taxi service allegedly with a US$10,000 inheritance from an uncle. They expanded their commercial activity and eventually relocated to Cochabamba in 1989, establishing themselves as one of the first inmobiliarias in the area. Once in Cochabamba, they acquired other businesses, including an air shuttle service, entertainment lounges, a TV channel, slowly establishing a name for themselves as savvy businessmen and "capturing the trust of approximately 15,000 investors" who handed over a total of US$9 million (CEDOIN 1991, 36). FINSA offered its investors interest rates of 6 percent compounded monthly.

In 1991 things slowly began to fall apart. The high interest rates offered raised suspicions from the United States Drug Enforcement Agency, and several investigations were undertaken to determine the legality of these operations. Two of the pilots hired by the Arévalo brothers were accused of trafficking drugs, and the company was forced to cease its services while a more thorough investigation took place. Assets were frozen and thousands of investors were deprived of the monthly income on which they came to depend. These actions led to widespread demonstrations against the government and general popular support for the Arévalo brothers, who had gone underground, claiming to fear for their lives. FINSA categorically denied any involvement with the narcotics trade. The money owed to the investors was never returned, and Nelson Arévalo was found shot in his car in September 1991. The circumstances and people surrounding his death were never clearly identified.

Rosalía's Loss

Rosalía had been among the thousands of people in Cochabamba who lost their savings in the inmobiliarias scam. Unlike most, however, she spoke freely and openly about her experience. She placed her money in FINSA and Multiactiva in hopes of collecting the robust annual interest rates promised (more than four times what the legitimate banks could offer). Shortly after Rosalía deposited her money the inmobiliaria crashed, leaving the investors (mainly poor people trying to maximize their savings) in the cold. Rosalía had dreamed of owning her own house, but when she lost the money, that dream became a very remote possibility. Rosalía recalled the day she heard about FINSA's financial problems:

> I was coming back from Cochabamba when on the radio I heard an announcement saying that anyone who had their money in FINSA or Multiactiva should go to the offices because there were problems. The next day, I went very early and they told me that it was a false alarm. Well, three days later, things stayed like that [the company folded]. They told me that I lost all of my money and that they had killed him, the boss [Arévalo], and that he had jewels on all his fingers, that he had a gold watch and a fat bracelet, a fat gold chain around his neck. I saw it. Earlier [before he was killed] I had gone to his office and I went to him and knelt down in front of him begging him to please return my money. "*Señora*," he said, "I'm sorry, I will do everything possible to help you, to help the poor people." He told me . . . they were going to have to figure out where the money was. . . . I told him I took the bread out of my children's mouths to invest, I took away from them to save. Three days after I talked to him they killed him. Three days exactly. I never went back after that.

The economic devastation unraveled by the scheme affected people of all classes, not just the "gullible" campesinos. For Rosalía, the battering that she suffered at the hands of her husband was severely intensified when she lost her savings. "My husband never let up and kept telling me how stupid I had been for putting the money in that inmobiliaria. He made me 'eat' that night and day (*me hacia comer eso dia y noche*), and he mistreated me a lot." It had been Rosalía who persuaded her husband to invest the money. She convinced him that they could live off each month's interest and continue to invest a few dollars each month to increase their savings. In addition, she told him: "Let's try to save while the children are small, because when they are older they will be more demanding asking for this and that, and it's going to be more difficult." She then said to me, "And for what did we deposit it?! All the money went to the water [to waste]! [¡*Todo el dinero se fue al agua!*]"

"How was it," I asked, "that you didn't get sick during such rage and sorrow?"

She paused briefly and then, placing her hands on her stomach, she replied:

> I was pregnant at the time with my youngest son. I say that maybe all of my rage and sorrow, I passed on to him because all I did was cry—I ate lunch, I cried, I ate breakfast, I cried, I'd go out, I'd cry. Because I used to be fat back then [*yo era gorda*], but since that happened, I was so upset I just kept losing weight and then my son was born. And now look at me, I am just like this. I am no longer fat. I used to be fat. Because of all that, I suffered from preoc-

cupation a lot back then. . . . I didn't have a single piece of bread to eat and that was my main preoccupation.

Rosalía was weakened by the emotional and financial stress she was under. This is referenced in her lamentations about her weight loss. Being what might be considered slightly "overweight" by Western standards was a marker of health in Punata. She noted, however, that at the time of her losses she was strong enough so as to not have a miscarriage—a common occurrence in pregnant women who feel intense rage or sorrow, according to many women I interviewed. Her son, however, came to suffer from debilidad, and his was seen as a constitutional debilidad that developed when Rosalía passed all her suffering on to him in utero. After Rosalía exhausted all possibilities of gaining her money back, she found herself helpless and desperate. Although the sorrow and despair that she experienced did not make her sick, she believed that it had permanently affected her child. That she did not fall ill indicates the strength of her own body but underscores the vulnerability of the child inside her who received the brunt of the stress. Unlike Elisa, who could treat her infant and deflect blame for the child's onset of arrebato, Rosalía's child's debilidad had no therapeutic solution—no medicines would ever alleviate his condition. Fernando was permanently affected with debilidad while in the womb. Just as Rosalía was helpless in the face of the bank scam, no solution could help protect her child from the long-term effects of her suffering.

One additional factor must be taken into account in trying to understand the salience of discourses of debilidad. Debilidad is a social marker. When one person over another was pointed out as débil, there was an implicit understanding that this person suffered and had a hard life, was let down, neglected, or mistreated (often unfairly in the eyes of the sufferer) by family, community members, or life. When an infant was pointed out as débil, however, it marked a mother's past suffering. As such, she might not be as harshly criticized for her inability to adequately address her child's ailments and susceptibility.

Maternal emotions in the context of Punata were seen to have an important influence on infant health. Close attention to the discursive and embodied dimensions of emotions permit a more comprehensive understanding of how emotions are subjectively felt to affect health in Bolivia. To focus solely on power relations and the expression of emotions and their effects on health does not help us understand the mechanisms through which emotions are embodied. Similarly, to divorce an understanding of the embodiment of emotions from contexts of the social and economic realities unleashed by the neoliberal reforms (including unregulated markets and encouragement to advance oneself) and the effort to launder the money produced by the cocaine industry presents a myopic understanding of distress and health.

The short- and long-term effects of maternal emotions on infant health as seen in the manifestation of debilidad and arrebato reveal that these ailments signal tensions in the social landscape: among neighbors, family members, co-workers, or as a result of failed efforts to improve one's economic conditions. Debilidad and arrebato are salient and exacerbated during times of social crisis, community or familial conflicts, and economic hardship. These were the felt bodily effects of the reforms and were among the ways that moral actors rationalized the radical economic changes happening around them. The problems surrounding individuals, households, and communities with root causes in the materiality of poverty, unemployment, domestic violence, high rates of alcoholism, or economic recession were merely a few of the factors that led to debilidad and arrebato in infants.

The body and its ailments communicate polysemous messages of disappointment, neglect, economic scarcity, and marital or household conflict. Many of these messages are imbued with moral value. Furthermore, these ailments and symptoms may help structure social obligations, social roles, and the relationship between and among people. By evoking a particular illness category, people might receive greater empathy and support from those around them. To say a child has arrebato is to signal that the mother may be suffering from economic hardship or from domestic violence. To claim a child has debilidad can signal past maternal distress, deflecting blame from current difficulties in caring for one's children. Such signals, in turn, can lead to community interference. A husband, for instance, may be told not to be so harsh with his wife. A neighbor might share their crops with those who did not fare so well in a particular season. A city cousin may offer a harried mother free room and board for a child attending an urban school or university. In other instances, however, the very same diagnosis affecting infants can unleash an intricate politics of mother-blame, which can be negotiated and contested by women (see Tapias 2006a). To evoke a particular infant illness term communicates not only an array of symptoms but also hints at some of the emotional origins of these symptoms and ailments, and indicates who might be at "fault" for these emotions in the first place, such as faltering banks, a delinquent car buyer, or a mother with "uncontrollable" emotions.

4

Anxious Ambitions and the Financing of Tranquility

In conditions of economic hardship and recession, it is sometimes easy to overlook the fact that some people still manage to fare well. The terrain for economic success in Punata, however, was decidedly uneven, and for those who did experience relative prosperity, their success came at significant social costs. While medical anthropologists have examined the negative health effects neoliberal reforms have had on the poor through a focus on structural violence, they have paid less attention to the other violences people may experience, even if those individuals do not find themselves living under the same economic adversity as truly destitute populations (Farmer 1996). While throughout my fieldwork it was clear that the poor were hardest hit by the reforms, the middle classes also suffered different forms of distress (Masseroni and Sauane 2003; Kleinman 2000). One such manifestation of distress was the increased anxiety about envy and sorcery.

Concerns over envy and sorcery were engendered by the economic and political transformations Bolivia was undergoing as it engaged in neoliberal capitalism and as the state sought to restructure its relationship to world markets and its citizens. From the perspective of a neoliberal economic agenda, sound governing and sound policies are rooted in economic growth, access to private property, and self-reliance—not in dependency or the welfare state (Cotoi 2011). The economic policies encouraged increased competition between Bolivian and international markets and the retrenchment of state benefits. Simultaneously, the policies had more local effects, as market women competed with one another and also had to contend with a decrease in social services and with an exploding informal market sector. While market shelves displayed cheap products from China and food goods from Chile and Peru, the ability of people to prosper under these conditions was unequally distributed. One concrete effect of this inequality was that neighbors compared themselves to neighbors, so increasing pressures were felt in households to conceal any hint of success.

My focus in this chapter is on the experiences of a particular echelon of the market: members of a group of more prosperous career chola and mestiza market women. I examine how these women sought to mitigate their fears of envy and sorcery through their religious devotion to an image of Saint James known as "Tata Bombori." Tata Bombori is considered the patron saint of healers and sorcerers. The venerated image of the saint is located in a small church in the town of Bombori, Potosí, but replicas of his image are present in many households in Punata. Each June and July, at the height of the Bolivian winter, thousands of Andean and mestizo men and women from all over the country and from as far away as Peru and Argentina undertake a pilgrimage to the Catholic shrine. Pilgrims make the expensive journey in an effort to garner the saint's protection and to alleviate their physical and emotional suffering.

Figure 3. Image of Bombori

Those who pray to Bombori often fear or seek protection from envy, believe they are ensorcelled (or at risk of being hexed), or find their problems or illnesses to be a "lost cause." The trip to Bombori, for those who can afford it, is often a last-chance effort to address their maladies or ill fortune. In addition to visiting the shrine, many pilgrims go to Bombori because during the festivities numerous traditional healers, coca readers, and ritualists from all over Bolivia "set up shop" in the streets and are available for consultations and healing sessions. The pilgrimage thus often serves as one preventive or curative strategy in people's long quest for well-being across different health sectors.

The narratives of Bombori devotees highlight the uneasy and embodied ways in which women reconciled their fears of being the object of envy with an emergent subjectivity that included desires for the prosperity and wealth promised by the Bolivian state. As detailed in chapter 1, the neoliberal economic reforms fostered free trade, encouraged privatization of many industries, and also propagated notions of individualism, "doing well," and competing in the market economy. While entrepreneurship, self-reliance, and independence were valued and encouraged at the state level, public displays of ambition locally were viewed with ambivalence. When wealth was displayed, the act was often seen as an incentive or justification for friends and family to ask for favors and money. When these requests were ignored or went unfulfilled, the groundwork was laid for envy to flourish. The apparent (but not always secure) economic success of certain market women often indexed them in the eyes of the community as individuals who privileged their own self-interests, eroding in the process the local moral codes regarding social and material reciprocity. The rituals performed either during the pilgrimage or through devotion at home provided women with both public and intimate avenues to construct a strong religious identity and also obtain protection for their entrepreneurial endeavors. In the following pages I examine how devotion to Bombori was one mechanism to manage the social costs of success. The pilgrimage and hosting of local fiestas in the saint's honor were a way to "finance" tranquility, secure a pathway for future economic success, and mitigate the envy that might flourish because of entrepreneurial activities.

Entrepreneurship among market women was not a new phenomenon, nor did it begin only after the implementation of the economic reforms. Several scholars have discussed the savvy and astuteness of Andean market women (Buechler, Buechler, and Buechler 1998; Seligmann 2004; Weismantel 2001). What had changed during my fieldwork, however, was an economic crisis that created increased competition between vendors, precarious living conditions, and erosion of people's ability to make ends meet (Gill 2000). In Bolivia and throughout the Andes the reforms profoundly rearticulated the contours of social, community, and familial relations across class, gender, and ethnic lines. For example, in some households male unemployment caused by privatization was accompanied by the formation of new gender roles as women became the primary income earners; imported products flooding market shelves created new desires and longings for items that were not always accessible to those with modest incomes; loans between individuals could not always be repaid, causing conflicts between neighbors; and increased parental migration to neighboring countries left children under the supervision of grandparents or other relatives. The reforms thus fueled a restructuring of daily life and reconfigured community and familial interactions (Menjívar 2003).

Privatization, reliance on the free market, and the retrenchment of social services were all hailed as the key ingredients to catalyze Bolivia's economic transformation. These policies, as discussed in chapter 1, set the stage for inciting a rapid increase in the already prominent informal economy. Women and men previously employed turned either to informally selling food products and staples from their homes or to street and market vending as the only viable economic opportunities within their reach (Agadjanian 2003). The growth in the informal economy helped absorb a considerable portion of laid-off workers across the country into the workforce and also provided an avenue to make up for incomes lost in the household. In Punata this growth in the informal economy was visible as more women set up stands in the central market or began to sell products from their own homes. While these home businesses may not have had the same abundance of clients as the central market, they enjoyed a steady trickle of customers who were able to avoid a trip to the town center. The increased numbers of in-home vendors as well as itinerant vendors in the central market placed numerous stresses on already established market vendors who now had to compete for clients with these newer sellers. The experiences of these established market vendors are the focus of this chapter.

There is a tendency to the view market women as a uniform and undifferentiated group. While market women are often referred to as "*las cholas del Mercado*" (the cholas of the market), not all women identify as such or don a pollera, the multilayered cotton, silk, or velveteen skirt (de la Cadena 1995; Weismantel 2001). The market is greatly stratified and fragmented, and there are many ethnic, class, and age hierarchies represented. Scholarship on market women by Weismantel (2001) in Ecuador, Seligmann (1998, 2004) in

Peru, and Buechler, Buechler, and Buechler (1998) in Bolivia has sought to complicate these essentializing views of the informal economy. Seligmann notes, for example, that "informal economies are not homogeneous—within them different occupational categories, such as that of the market women, are also remarkably differentiated" (Seligmann 1998, 67). This differentiation is readily visible in Punata, where social relations between market women are often laden with conflict and tension. Many schoolteachers and administrators who formerly enjoyed recognition in the community were laid off during the educational and administrative decentralization reforms, which began as early as 1995. As they resorted to selling products in the market to supplement (or at times, replace) their incomes, their economic "demotion" caused inner and social conflict, and they frequently had to swallow their pride. These women often considered themselves "professionals" and superior to the stereotypical uneducated market women. The downward mobility of these women added a layer of palpable resentment with which older marker women had to contend. Thus, regular tensions arose between those long-time market vendors who were relatively successful and those who were struggling.

The Punata market was marked by several social hierarchies that came into play in social interactions. For example, the scale of a market woman's enterprise influenced her position and possible prestige in this hierarchy. A person had to make a larger economic investment and have greater access to capital to be able to sell meat, for example, than to sell fruit juices. Purchasing cattle, pork, lamb, or chicken also required an investment in refrigeration. The breadth of a market women's clientele also significantly influenced her position in the market. If a market woman had contracts with restaurant and hotel owners, she could count on a more reliable source of income that was supplemented by the daily profits she could manage to make through small sales. The breadth of her clientele was often linked to the number of years she had worked in the market, how extensive her compadrazgo ties were, and whether she inherited clients from retired relatives. The longer one worked in the market, the greater the likelihood one could develop relationships with clients and make them into *caseras,* regular clients who were under an unspoken obligation to purchase goods from particular sellers offering the products. In exchange, these clients received other "perks" and incentives to continue the relationship: a little extra merchandise when they made a purchase (known as a *yapa*), flexible payment options, and prompt attention before non-casera clients.

Two key issues distinguished successful from struggling market women: the length of time they had worked in the central market and whether they had a *puesto fijo* (a fixed market post) or were *ambulantes* (itinerant). The more established market women had fixed market posts and tended to come from families who had worked in the market for several generations. These women belonged to and paid dues to the vendor's association (*sindicato*) (Buechler, Buechler, and Buechler 1998). However, even within this group there could be marked gradations of wealth, depending on how much overhead the vendor stocked and how much money she managed. In contrast, the *ambulantes* sold goods in different places each day. On some days, these women had literally to squeeze themselves between regular vendors. They set up their woven cloths on the floor and sold smaller piles of tomatoes or peppers, school supplies, spices, fruit juices, and other goods, often under the protests of women who paid full dues. Sometimes they stocked their products in wheelbarrows, which they pushed around town. In addition, vendors in the weekly regional market on Tuesdays, which attracted vendors from as far away as the department of Santa Cruz, competed with even the most successful market women, who complained of pitiful sales.

The economic stratification between vendors was also visible in the very "geography" of the Punata market. The stalls of meat vendors, for example, were situated along the north and south walls of the market square, under the shade of the building's eaves, a step above the other stalls. A tile counter stacked with different cuts of meat separated the vendor from her clients. The meat sellers were arranged in two rows facing one another, but, as a whole, the vendors faced the center of the market. This meant that the women seated in the outermost edge faced the center of the market while the women seated directly in front of them had their backs facing the center of the market. It was this latter position that, for some, was the more desirable position. At their own will those positioned here could either face the center of the market or turn their bodies in ways that granted them a little more privacy. In either position, however, they had a good overview of all the activities in their vicinity.

The east and west sides of the market were occupied by the canned-goods vendors, whose overhead could also be quite high. While they did not enjoy the elevated position shared by the meat vendors, they still had a good overview of the market. The fruit and vegetable sellers, as well as spice and dry-good vendors, sold in the middle of the market. Because most of these stalls were exposed to the sun and rain, vendors set up white cloth parasols for protection. Their products were among the cheapest items in the market. Some of these women had fixed posts and tended to sit on low stools by their produce. Many did not have fixed posts; they set out blankets and displayed their products on the floor. Walking through the market, one got the feeling of being under constant surveillance. As I'd make my daily journey through the market, I'd hear a canon of voices luring me to their stands: "Comprame caserita," "Comprame waway," "¿Que cosita quieres mamitay?" "Rantiway, waway." "Buy from me, caserita," "Buy from me, my child," "What would you like, little mother?" "Buy from me, my child." Together, these voices, laden with affection, sought to persuade customers to purchase goods. In the course of a day women knew who was selling well and who was not, who a vendor's regular clients were and when they came to the market. When a conflict erupted, most people in the market knew about it. When two market women argued, they could not do so privately. Indeed, the market's layout created fertile ground for envy to flourish. My concern is to explore the tensions and troubles that the more successful women experienced with other less successful market women, as well as with one another, and how they mitigated their fears of envy and jealousy that arose from their relative success.

Envy and Embodied Manifestations of Distress

Concerns about envy and sorcery and the risks they pose to health played a key role in the local embodied understandings of distress in Punata. Envy is seen as an "equal opportunity" emotion, in that anyone, regardless of race, class, or gender, could be vulnerable to its effects. In illnesses caused by envy, it was the envious who brought on trouble by enlisting the services of a *yatiri* (a healer that could harm as well as heal) to place a hex on the envied person. When Father Crecensio, the parish priest featured in chapter 2, beseeched his parishioners not to repay evil with evil, he was pleading for them not to cyclically resort to sorcery. Even though anyone could be the victim of another's envy, rumors and gossip about how it was directed at the middle classes abounded. Both men and women gossiped, and as they participated in this talk, they subtly revealed their allegiances and judged who was at fault for the conflicts fueling envy (Glass-Coffin 1992; Van Vleet 2003). Stories circulated about domestic workers who tried to poison the members of the households where they worked; about laborers who resorted to sorcery because they resented their bosses for denying them cash advances or for paying poor wages; about jealous neighbors who envied others for building new houses or for not extending loans when a fellow community member was in need. Among market women the fear of being the object of such envy was pervasive. Graciela, a woman who sold incense and other items for rituals, commented: "Here in Punata, people are very envious; they are mean, jealous. Here, for any small reason they hex you. Here people see that someone is working well and they get all envious." Similarly, Vera (who sold breakfast beverages) was reported to the market authorities by one of her co-workers for "spiking" a hot drink for some laborers. She was consequently fined, and Vera complained about the envy of the woman who denounced her, saying, "In this town there never is a lack of envious people." Vera started circulating rumors of her own concerning alleged unhygienic practices her accuser had in the preparation of her beverages. A meat vendor, Teresa, told me her neighbor was extremely envious of her for selling chicha (corn beer) out of her home. Her neighbor, who also owned a chichería and was concerned about increased competition and selling less herself, told Teresa, "You already have an income from selling meat; don't sell chicha anymore." Apart from the widespread view these women shared that envy was all around, they also shared certain social characteristics: they were seen as successful market women viewed by others as ambitious.

Emotions and the Ambivalence of Ambition

As I have argued throughout this book, Punateña men and women associate numerous illnesses and ailments with economic hardship and the emotions that accompany such circumstances. More successful market women also linked their health problems to emotions, although they did not experience the same economic duress. The rage and sorrow they felt was often related to the disjuncture between how they viewed themselves and how they thought community members perceived them. Market women spoke of their strong work ethic and the sacrifices they had to endure to ensure economic stability for their families, education for their children, and respect in their communities. Meanwhile, those who envied them often viewed these market women as ambitious and selfish. The economic prosperity of certain market women thus came with significant social costs.

Ambition carried with it several negative connotations in Punata and was viewed with considerable ambivalence (for other examples of the ambivalence that surrounds new forms of wage labor, see Mills 1997; Ong 1991; and Richman 2005). To say that a person—male or female—was ambitious was not meant as a compliment or seen as an index of someone who worked hard to improve his or her lot. To call someone *ambicioso/ambiciosa* was deprecating. *Ambiciosos/ambiciosas* were seen as people who were not content with the possibilities they had in front of them. Mariana, a woman who owned a small store that operated from her home, explained: "How do I describe someone who is ambitious? They are people that are never satisfied with what they have; they are ambitious. In other words, having [economic stability] they always want more. They don't consider others." Their ambition thus drives them to seek out more property, wealth, or prestige even if that choice may hurt others in the process. An ambiciosa was seen as someone who forgot the responsibilities that came with reciprocity and who privileged self-interest and advancement. Flora, an established market women and who herself was often seen as ambitious, offered, for example, to help her young daughter-in-law, Susana, establish herself in the market, to set up and stock her stand, but Susana politely refused. Susana wanted to emigrate to Spain to seek out employment. Her cousin, who had already emigrated, had told her that work caring for the elderly was readily available. Flora was baffled that Susana could decline her generous offer and finally said to me, *"¡Es pues ambiciosa! ¿Como no va querer que alguien le arregle un puesto?"* "She's just ambitious! How could she not want someone to arrange a stand for her?" Flora herself had inherited her market stall from her own mother-in-law and had been very grateful. In light of the appreciation Flora had for her own mother-in-law, Susana's refusal was particularly painful. Rather than interpret Susana's initiative to emigrate positively, Flora saw her refusal as a statement that market vending was not "good enough." Having a great opportunity in front of her, Susana wanted more. She declined her mother-in-law's generous offer and risked the uncertainties that she might face in Spain, such as discrimination or the inability to find steady work.

It is not surprising that there was uneasiness and considerable concern about being viewed as ambitious. This apprehension stemmed from the tensions that emerged from adeptly grappling and negotiating with two competing discourses that shaped how Punateñas understood their relationship to others: one that drew upon "traditional" rules of reciprocity and a more recent "asocial" approach of state-promoted capitalist entrepreneurship, which encouraged people to *avanzar*, advance themselves and become modern by earning money and having the means to consume modern commodities (Lind 2003; Sikkink 2001; VanVleet 2003, 2008; see also Greene 2001 for an examination of *"salir adelante,"* getting ahead, in Mexico). Successful market women (and others) were seduced by this latter discourse and were able to demonstrate their ability to "avanzar" through their own hard work and initiative. Nonetheless, they were still very much dependent on and/or indebted to social networks, some members of which were not faring as well. Because of dependence on social networks, successful market women could not be entirely self-reliant. They were continuously aware of their vulnerability to malicious gossip and envy, and so they continuously feared for their health and well-being. Interacting with others as they aspire to improve their social and economic conditions entailed the ability to negotiate these tensions with skill and find zones of comfort that enable them to engage with traditional networks. The narratives of Marta and Flora, to which I now turn, aptly illustrate this dexterity.

Marta and Flora were two of many devotees of Tata Bombori in Punata. Both were women with established market stands, and both were constantly worried about sorcery and envy. At age thirty, Marta was heavily in debt but had a fully stocked stand and was trying to establish herself as a respected market vendor. She carefully nourished relationships with clients, attended fiestas in town, agreed to forge new compadrazgo ties, and tried to get along with other market women. Flora, at age forty-nine, was already established and by local standards quite prosperous. She had built two homes (one for herself and another for her eldest daughter and two grandsons) and had put five sons through trade schools at different times. For both women, their devotion to Bombori helped appease their anxieties about being targets of envy and enabled them to continue pursuing their business endeavors. Their cases illustrate that the stability of their social interactions and social relations were not inoculated against the difficult choices they made as they enacted the demands of capitalist entrepreneurship. I begin with the case of Marta who I accompanied on the pilgrimage to the shrine of Bombori. I then turn to Flora's story; she had undertaken the pilgrimage years earlier and in 2006 began to host a local fiesta in honor of the saint. Her devotion actively continued through the services of a local healer.

The Pilgrimage to Bombori and the Financing of Tranquility

Although people visit the shrine of Bombori throughout the year, the main pilgrimage and accompanying rituals take place in July and constitute expensive undertakings. In addition to transportation costs, a pilgrim had also to provide ample libations and candles, pay for accommodations, and hire the services of a healing guide. Many people saved for months (sometimes years) to prepare for the trip. While devotees viewed it as a religious experience undertaken with faith, the pilgrimage was also seen as an "investment" toward future tranquility. Tranquility is an idealized state that emerges as the antithesis of states of emotional turmoil, stress, and discomfort (Hammer 1997; Low 1985). The pursuit of tranquility is a lifelong and continuous process, and only brief contextual moments of it are enjoyed. When undertaken with faith, the pilgrimage was said to help even the most hopeless cases of sorcery.

Marta decided to undertake the pilgrimage in search of protection and tranquility. At first sight, Marta was an upwardly mobile market woman. She wore Western clothing and sold *viveres*: food staples like flour, sugar, eggs, spices, rice, noodles, and canned goods. Marta was the eldest of six siblings and had a ten-year-old son, Joaquín. She began working at age eight, helping her mother who owned one of the restaurants in the market. Marta was the only sibling to work in the market; the other five had been sent to college or trade school. She often referred to herself as *sin profesión*, "without a profession," and this was a source of conflict between Marta and her mother. During arguments Marta regularly reminded her mother, "You had your children study at my expense" (*A cargo de mi has hecho estudiar a tus hijos*). Marta would have liked to have studied but, as the eldest, was expected to help her mother care for the younger siblings, and eventually her labor was also needed in their restaurant.

Marta's driving goal in life was to provide her son Joaquín with the opportunity she had been denied: to study and obtain a profession. *Con eso, estaré realizada*: "With that," she said, "I will feel accomplished/fulfilled." While wealth was clearly linked with being modern, attaining an education was also a vital gateway to getting ahead in Bolivia and the Andes (Seligman 1989, 2004; Weismantel 2001). While Marta had her own market stand to tend, she continued to help with the restaurant and often had to leave her stand briefly to supervise the helpers. Marta never stood still while selling in her stand; she was always shelling peas or fava beans, chopping carrots, or mincing parsley for the cooks. She continuously complained about the restaurant's workers, all of whom were cholas, whom she often saw as lazy and needing constant supervision. "They don't want to work," she would repeatedly complain.

Marta's market stand was always very well stocked, and neighboring vendors often sent customers to her if they didn't have a particular product. Privately, however, she remarked that she was heavily in debt. This was echoed by her close friend, who commented, "Why does she keep buying things if she already owes so much money?" Not only did she owe money to a local cooperative, but Marta also participated in the market's *pasanaku*.[1] The pasanaku was a rotating credit association in which a group of market women each contributed a fixed amount of money each week to a communal pool; the lump sum was then given to one of the members of the group on a rotating basis until all had their turn. When Marta's turn came to receive the sum of money, she chose to stock up on more products (fearing future price increases) rather than pay off her debts. So while Marta availed herself of "traditional" sources of mutual aid, she took this income as an opportunity to invest in her business. Marta was continuously concerned about other people's envy as well as her multiple creditors' wrath at her failure to pay back her debts. She worried the former might resort to sorcery because they coveted her apparent affluence as visible in her well-stocked stall and was also continuously preoccupied that her creditors might resort to sorcery out of anger. Actual or perceived prosperity could lead to sorcery but so too could failure to prosper and meet one's debt obligations. Lena, the daughter of another market woman, explained: "People can ensorcell you out of envy, but you are also afraid of sorcery when you are afraid of revenge. My family, for instance, owes lots of money, and we're always thinking that someone is going to hex us. Everyday when we leave the house, we all rustle the leaves of the *ruda* bush for protection."[2]

Marta decided to undertake the pilgrimage to Bombori along with her mother to garner the saint's protection and mitigate her fear of sorcery. A few months prior to the pilgrimage she had a conflict with another market woman who was a close friend. They no longer spoke, and since the conflict Marta had noticed a decline in her sales and mounting debt. The stream of bad luck was disconcerting to her, so since a group of pilgrims were already planning to undertake the journey, she decided to join them. Later, during the pilgrimage, she explained why people undertake the journey:

> Everyone here comes to be healed or to be protected. Between brothers and sisters[3] we harm one another; we do each other evil and that's why we come to Bombori. So he can protect us. People from all over Bolivia come to Bombori. . . . Problems are never lacking, there is envy, people are evil, there is always maliciousness . . . and the lazier people are—the more envious they are! . . . When people see that you are doing ok, that you are making money, then they place a hex on you. Even if you have worked hard for it, people who are envious and people who want to do you harm are never lacking.

Other women who felt that they worked hard their entire lives only to be compensated with other people's envy echoed these sentiments. Marta's statement displayed her frustration regarding the social costs of her hard work.

Her diligence and work ethic were not rewarded with advancement and upward mobility but instead stimulated envy and conflict with her peers. The pilgrimage thus unfolds in a shifting economic landscape that pits intimates and acquaintances against one another.

Several key events during the pilgrimage clearly articulated the centrality that envy occupied in the eyes of the devotees: the purification rituals that took place upon departure and arrival to the religious site; a cathartic and emotional ceremony on the first full night of the pilgrimage when petitions were made to Tata Bombori; and a more subdued request for goods and good fortune prior to departure. I turn to these events to illustrate my points.

Departures

Once a pilgrim decided to undertake the voyage from Punata, their departure was a very public event. On the evening when pilgrims undertook their trip, family members and friends accompanied them to a central meeting point. Pilgrims convened in a large area (often in the courtyard of the guiding healer's home) with their baggage: several blankets for protection against cold nights, baskets of food, beverages, colorful tied-up *awayos* holding clothing, hundreds of candles and sometimes pots and pans to cook with along the way. Pilgrims and family members huddled together around the courtyard and talked about past pilgrimages undertaken and shared chicha as they waited for the bus. The mood was festive, and there was eager anticipation in the air. As departure time approached, family members showered their loved ones with *mistura* (confetti) and wished them luck. They sent the pilgrims off with a *qoqawi* for the ride (a snack sack with empanadas, beef jerky, fruit, bread, cheese, fava beans, a thermos with hot herbal tea, and other food items) as well as more candles to be lit at the religious site on their behalf.

While waiting for departure, all pilgrims underwent the first purification ritual. Two similar ritual cleansings took place during their journey at several Stations of the Cross located on the outskirts of Bombori, on the main dirt road that leads to the town. My field notes describe these rituals:

> When I arrive at Doña Benita's house (the healer and guide who will accompany us on the trip), Marta, Doña Emma, and Doña Vera [the women I am accompanying on the pilgrimage] are already gathered with their respective families. Aside from them, there are about one hundred other people assembled, including other pilgrims and their families and friends. The confetti- and chicha-covered courtyard

feels crowded as people stand close together, chatting. I see Marta seated on a stack of at least fifteen wool blankets and wonder if I'm underdressed. They scoff at my thin winter jacket and sleeping bag but then tell me not to worry, as they have plenty of blankets for everyone. I am accompanied by my comadre. As the closest person I have to "family" in town, she sees it as her responsibility to send me off as I undertake the trip. We stand around talking and waiting, but I'm not sure for what.

Doña Benita (our guide) emerges from a room at the back of the courtyard and calls us. I am poked in the side by Marta and told that it is our turn. I had not noticed that throughout the evening, different groups enter the rear room and reemerge shortly after. The four of us—Marta, Doña Emma (Marta's mother), Doña Vera (Doña Emma's comadre) and I—join hands and make our way through the crowd toward the back of the courtyard. We enter the room, and Doña Benita closes the door behind us. Along with a fifth woman I do not know, we are told to kneel before Doña Benita. She conducts the full purification ritual on each of us individually, one after the other.

I observe as she conducts the ritual on Marta. Marta is asked to exhale three times on to a ball of coarse wool. The healer takes the wool and "measures" Marta's head with the yarn: from ear to ear and from nape to forehead. With the yarn bunched up in her hands she makes the sign of the cross over Marta's chest. Doña Benita then stretches out the strand of yarn and wraps the ends around each of her hands and moves it along Marta's body. Doña Benita forcefully rips the yarn in two and sternly murmurs "¡Lloqsiy Envidia!" "Leave, Envy!"; again: "¡Lloqsiy Maldad!" "Leave, badness [evil]!"; again: "¡Lloqsiy Diablo! ¡Lloqsiy Satanás!" "Leave, Devil! Leave, Satan!" Praying quietly, she ends her ritual in Quechua by saying "Tata Bombori, bless her." Doña Benita rolls up the broken pieces of wool into a ball, has Marta exhale over them three times, and saves the strands in a plastic bag, which she will later burn in an offering. Doña Benita completes the rituals on each one of us, and as we are about to exit Vera tells her I come from the United States and that it is my first time visiting Bombori. Doña Benita smiles, welcomes me, and tells me Bombori is a very miraculous saint. She blesses me and says: "Tata Bombori protect her. Tata doctor, protect her."

* * *

Doña Benita cleansed us so that any evil, envy, or meanness shackling our *ánimos* (souls) is left behind. It is said that this enables pilgrims to undertake the voyage with an open heart so that the pilgrimage has the greatest potential to be a success. As we emerged into the courtyard once again, we noticed several other market women we knew who came to bid us farewell and good luck. Each one brought with him or her petitions for protection from envy and sorcery embodied in white candles. Each candle had previously been rubbed over the bodies of the petitioners and their initials carved into the wax. Between the four of us we had more than five hundred candles to take to Bombori. Shortly after 7:00 P.M., we were told by the bus driver to start loading onto the bus. About an hour later, once all pilgrims were aboard, the bus started its slow departure from town. Family members and friends walked along the bus for half a block and then were left behind and waved us off. They lit firecrackers and fireworks announcing and celebrating our group's departure.

The first few hours of the bus ride were animated by people's chatter and by music played on the bus's stereo. Silence fell over the bus temporarily, followed by laughter, after the driver played a recording of *taquipayanakus*, hilarious duets sung in Quechua and Spanish, usually peppered by sexual lyrics. During the journey I talked to Doña Vera, who was undertaking the journey in search of tranquility and peace. As we talked about the pilgrimage, she told me:

> I was told that if you are truly ensorcelled, upon your return the person who is doing this to you will die or suffer a horrible illness. But if you are not ensorcelled then nothing happens to them. Nothing happens and you too can have your tranquility. But you must go with faith, you must go asking for Tata Bombori's protection, and ask that if you are hexed, he heal you.

Petitions

The first day at Bombori was spent finding accommodations and food, visiting the church and town, and attending a Mass toward the end of the evening. For several hours after the Mass, the pilgrims each lit the hundreds of candles sent with them and then spent time sharing coca leaves, cigarettes, and alcoholic beverages with other pilgrims in front of the church. Regardless of conflicts back home or class divisions among the pilgrims, no one turned down an offering of alcohol or drinks from anyone, no matter how humble the offer. United in their fear of sorcery, there was at first sight a temporary suspension of ethnic and class distinctions as people drank, smoked, and chewed coca together. But closer examination revealed that people clearly marked their class backgrounds through what they offered others to drink. While some could afford to buy only grain alcohol, which they might mix with Kool-Aid, others brought chicha or more costly wine or beer. Among our group Marta proudly pulled out a bottle of ready-made strawberry daiquiris, an index of her modern taste. People welcomed the opportunity to taste the sweetened beverage, and the drinking and exchanging continued for several more hours. The next phase of the pilgrimage is further illustrated in my field notes:

> At midnight the inebriated pilgrims are slowly ushered up a hill behind the church to ascend a Calvary upon which was stationed a large wooden cross. Once at the top of the hill, each person is instructed by Dona Benita to rub cotton or a rock over his or her body and to leave it with great faith at the foot of the large cross with the request for Tata Bombori. "This," Dona Benita explains, "cleanses your body from any curse it may be under." Marta and the other pilgrims are instructed to go around the cross three times on their knees. I don't have the endurance to tolerate the physical pain; I slowly stand up, hoping not to draw too much attention to myself. Tears begin to stream down Marta's cheeks; she and the other pilgrims are in pain as their knees are encrusted with the sharp edges of small pebbles and stones. While going around the cross, some shout out their respective sorrows and concerns in either Quechua or Spanish. In the most emotionally intense moment of the pilgrimage, men and women alike sob as they make their way around the cross. This is their opportunity to petition the saint for healing and for protection from an array of social problems and conflicts: envy from neighbors, unemployment, illnesses, domestic violence. Shouted problems are drowned out by mumbled prayers and the sobbing of the pilgrims, by healers praying around the shrine, and by people still exchanging alcohol and coca:

"Tata Bombori, please help me. Because of this truck I purchased, people are doing this to me. Please, Tata Bombori, please please help me. Help me!"

"My esteemed Tata Bombori, I am not an evil man, I am a good man! Why are they doing this to me? Help me Tata!"

"Tata! Please do not let people harm me. I work hard! I do not steal!"

"Our Lord of Bombori! Have mercy on me! I do not harm anyone!"
"Beloved Tata, what have I done to deserve this? Cure me Tata!"
"Tata, cure my sister, she has children and we need her!"

Marta, Doña Emma, and Doña Vera do not shout out their *penas*, their sorrows. Marta quietly murmurs her problems as the tears continue to flow. On her knees, she clutches her rosary, gently rubbing one bead after another as she prays and makes her petitions to the saint. Together the three women are certain that Tata Bombori will help them. Like them, thousands of pilgrims who come to Bombori each year deposit their faith in his ability to free them from the conflicts that continuously emerge in their changing society.

This evening was the most emotionally charged phase of the pilgrimage. Through the public airing of grievances, the pilgrims were united in the comfort they found in the saint. Everyone present believed themselves to be the victim of injustice, and devotion to Bombori helped assuage these feelings. As the night progressed, more and more pilgrims ascended the hill. People continued to drink and share coca and cigarettes, but hours later the cold and wind drove people down to town again to retire for the night.

Entrepreneurial Blessings

During the final day in Bombori a ritual took place wherein material requests, embodied in miniature replicas of the items being asked for, were blessed.[4] Here, pilgrims openly displayed their wishes for material commodities with the certainty that these items, if bestowed upon them, would have the blessing of Bombori. In the town plaza numerous vendors set up tables from which they sold minutely crafted, life-like replicas of commodities that permeated the desires of these Andean pilgrims: televisions, VCRs, computers, new cars, buses, and trucks; fully stocked market stands; new Spanish-style houses with tile rooftops, wrought iron balconies, and stucco walls; cattle and other farm animals; passports, airline tickets, visas, miniature stacks of dollar bills, small bags of produce, tiny burlap sacks of sugar, coffee, and flour; cell phones and numerous other consumer goods. The pilgrims circulated around these vendors, compared prices, and carefully selected the replicas that most closely resembled what they hoped one day to attain.

Doña Benita reconvened the pilgrims and directed them to the top of a hill, where she blessed the items purchased. Each pilgrim laid out the items desired and covered them in colorful streamers and confetti. The items were blessed by Doña Benita, and she also made generous offerings of chicha to the Pachamama. A walk among the pilgrims revealed their material wishes, many of which were beyond their own financial means. Marta purchased a miniature market stall, fully stocked with canned goods, sacks of flour, rice, and sugar, tiny packages of pasta, soups, and sauces, and the item most appealing to her: a tiny black telephone sitting upon a little orange crate which she would be able to rent out in the market on a per-call basis. "Look how beautiful this stand is—I want one exactly like it. I don't have a telephone in my stand. If you ask with faith, Our lord of Bombori, bestows." She urges me to run down the hill and purchase a replica of a dissertation for myself. "You'll see, you will have your thesis done in no time if you ask Tata Bombori for it." The pilgrims made their petitions with the peace of mind that although these material possessions could further fuel envy among their fellow Punateños, they had come with faith and had Tata Bombori's protection.

To many, the security they felt as a result of the pilgrimage was well worth the expense and time away from work. Our arrival back to Punata was just as noisy as our departure, announced with firecrackers, but this time at 3 A.M. Marta and the others spent the next few days telling people about the pilgrimage and sharing stories and copies of the anthropologist's pictures. The confidence in the protection provided by the pilgrimage to Bombori, however, slowly wore down with time as people faced new conflicts in their communities. In spite of this, people could continue to practice their devotion to the saint to reinvigorate and reestablish the protection. Such was the case with Flora, a successful meat vendor whose last pilgrimage to Bombori happened in 1988 but whose devotion remained steadfast.

Enduring Devotion

Flora occupied her market stand as a meat vendor for more than thirty years and throughout her career had also been active serving on several boards in her union. She learned her trade from her mother-in-law, from whom she inherited her stand. Although popular in the central market, Flora claimed that she could count her true and close friends on one hand. While at first glance her jovial and friendly personality gave the impression that she got along with everyone, she was always plagued by the fear of envy. "There is always envy," she would tell me. "No matter what you do, people are always envious." Her fear was further fueled by numerous enduring health problems she attributed to envy. Flora was one of the more successful meat vendors in the Punata market. She was *de pollera*, a sign that ethnically marked her as a chola. Indeed, at particular fiestas Flora often donned a new pollera, blouse, and shawl in the latest fashionable fabrics, displaying, in the process, her prosperity. Since many among the mestizo populations often consider cholas to be inferior to themselves, Flora's success was particularly unsettling to some (Weismantel 2001; Seligmann 2004).

Flora had an extensive network of caseras, compadres, and comadres whom she carefully attended to, as well as several contracts with restaurants in town. Over the years she managed to save enough money to send her children to college or trade school and also build a house and store for her eldest daughter, Mariana, a single mother of two boys who had attended two years of college but dropped out of school when she became pregnant with her first son. This Flora says, was one of her greatest disappointments in life. Flora often said she worked "only for her children," and her dream was for all of them to study, be "professionals," and have a better life than she had. Seligmann notes a similar finding among cholas in Peru: "If [cholas] make a profit, they tend to invest it in the education of their children, not in the expansion of their economic activities. Education thus becomes a form of social capital for them" (1989, 705). When Flora found out that Mariana had forfeited the education that she and Juan were trying to give her, she was deeply disillusioned. She recalled in one of our conversations what she had felt upon finding out her daughter was not attending classes.

> I felt a lot of anger because my daughter didn't study. I was angry ... I worked for nothing. Even my husband got sick for a month. He had no will to live, no strength, nothing, each day he cried, he cried all the time. I went to the university to ask about her grades and there were none, there was nothing, she wasn't going to class. That was my first upset. I worked in vain for three years; every fifteen days I used to send her money for rent, tuition, between 200 and 300 bolivianos. In three years how much money does that come out to? How could I not have gotten angry over this? I was furious—I cried, I cried a lot, I yelled at her until I was able to forget. I would remember and I would cry; now I remember and I feel great sorrow. I could have built a house with that money, purchased a car. But little by little I went forgetting. I almost had an *embolio*, [and] the doctor told me I needed to take care of myself or else I'd have an embolio. I lost all my will to live, I didn't even feel like selling, it was a huge disappointment, I wanted to just take off and go wherever. More than anything I had terrible headaches, I raged for six months, I had spent so much money [on her education].

To Flora, Mariana's dropping out of school was "an investment" gone bad. Mariana returned to Punata with her partner but after the birth of their second son he left them to search for work in Argentina. He seldom sent news and never sent money. As such, Flora was constantly preoccupied with how Mariana was going to earn a living; hence, one of the incentives to rebuild the house in which Mariana lived was also to improve the appearance of the store attached to it, from which Mariana could sell goods. The new house that Flora had built for Mariana was a great improvement over the house in which she originally lived—an adobe structure with pounded dirt floors. The new modern house was a two-story, concrete structure with plastered walls painted a light peach color, many glass windows, and a tiny decorative balcony outside the main bedroom, which overlooked the avenue. On the first floor they built a *tienda*, a small grocery store, which Mariana ran, equipped with two refrigerators and stocked with all kinds of products. I asked why Mariana didn't sell in the market with her but Flora stated she lacked the right "character." Flora was well versed in the affective labor and demand that was needed to be a successful seller. Frustration was a daily feature of work in the market. You had to have the right demeanor and ability to coax others to buy from you, and you often had to tolerate rudeness and verbal abuse (Hochschild 1983; Freeman 2011). Her response—"She just doesn't have the patience it takes"—revealed Flora's concerns that Mariana did not have what it took to compete successfully in the market.

Flora's prosperity did not come without physical and emotional costs. She worked seven days a week from 6:00 A.M. to 6:00 P.M., taking only Good Friday off (when most customers did not consume red meat). She saw her life as one of sacrifice. It troubled her that in spite of her hard work and feeling as if she earned everything she owned, people were envious of her. She knew that on some occasions others referred to her as "mean" or selfish. Because of her popularity she was often asked to become a godparent to a child or marriage, or to sponsor a fiesta. Financially, she could not accept all invitations, and she feared this fueled resentment as well. People regularly came to her doorstep with a plate of food in hand, as was custom when you requested someone to be a *madrina* (godmother). "People get really mad! Sometimes I pretend I'm not home so people can't ask me to become their comadre!" She was also known as someone who never loaned money to anyone but her children and, consequently, was seen as selfish and self-interested.[5] Flora, however, saw her refusal to lend money as fully justified. She was advised not to lend out money by a healer, more than ten years earlier. She recounts:

> In my house there was no money. . . . I didn't know where the money went. I just couldn't save so I decided to go have my coca leaves read. The healer told me [I had been cursed]: "Why did you lend someone money? They took that

money to the river and they released it in the current. And now your money, like water, leaves you."

It wasn't until she had the curse removed, at a considerable expense, that she began to be able to save money and build her own house. "Now I never lend any money to anyone; I already learned my lesson. I tell people I don't have anything. I never ask people to lend me anything and I never lend anything either." Other market vendors would often get upset when Flora refused to lend them something in the market (money, plastic bags, a barbeque grill, and so on) and saw that as an indicator of her lack of trust. While she would often explain her reasons for refusal, this would often further offend others for the mere suggestion that *they* might be capable of wishing her ill.

Flora's experience illustrates the tensions between social values, which dictated that she should help out her fellow community members, and her own drive to avanzar, to advance and prosper. Flora believed that one could lose one's luck (*suerte*) if one loaned out money, thus making it difficult to avanzar. On several occasions she would remind me:

> No one gave me what I have [including Mariana's house] as a gift. I'm up and about everyday at 4:00 A.M. Everyday. Sometimes I don't sleep. Sometimes I'm up past 10:00 P.M. at night hand washing clothing so I don't have to pay someone else to do it. All this so I can save money. But people are envious anyway.

In addition to the everyday conflicts, worries, and concerns about envy that she would have at the market, Flora also had conflicts with her next-door neighbor, Doña Elvira. From the onset of the construction of Mariana's house, Doña Elvira, a seventy-year-old Quechua woman who also owned a small grocery store in front of her house, raised objections and sought ways to stall or derail Flora's project. Doña Elvira feared that Mariana's new, bright, and modern store would readily lure away many of her own clients. Both women had been participating in the informal economy by selling items from their homes, but Doña Elvira was forecasting the economic strain she would face once Marina's store opened.

The initial dispute between Flora and Elvira was primarily over an adobe wall that divided their respective plots of land. Flora wanted to tear down the dividing wall to build a more modern concrete wall, which would also separate their respective back patios. Elvira objected, saying the wall was on her property and therefore could not be dismantled without her permission. Flora consulted with the local municipal office and they told her that the wall belonged to both parties. Initially, Flora wanted Doña Elvira to split the cost of the new wall with her but after weeks of discussion, she decided to pay for it herself: "What's the point of arguing with an older woman?" She explained to me that she must respect the older woman, that it would be inappropriate to argue with her, and that the other neighbors would criticize her rudeness. On other occasions, when Flora was feeling less sympathetic, she complained that her neighbor was a very difficult woman: "*¡Es bien fregada!*"

When construction workers tried to dismantle the wall, Doña Elvira protested and told them to stop construction until the dispute was legally resolved. Flora told the workers to begin building the other side of the house. A few months later, when the workers tried to dismantle the wall again, Elvira objected once more. Flora had secured the necessary permits and demonstrated that the wall belonged to both of them. Flora hoped that by evoking a legal discourse materialized in "official papers," their interactions might change from one of "elder to younger" to one between "property owners." Her efforts were unsuccessful. The construction workers, not wanting to take side in the feud (and thus leave themselves vulnerable to the wrath of one of the women), decided to stop construction until the personal conflict between them was resolved. As Flora tried to persuade her, the elderly neighbor persisted: "What makes you think that I am just going to give away my wall?" Flora reminded her the new wall would be beautiful, but Doña Elvira did not relent. Flora decided to build the new wall adjacent to the old one, losing in the process a half-meter of space to the elderly woman. "What can we do? We have to resign ourselves to this." Several weeks later, during one of my interviews with her, Flora recalled her encounter with Doña Elvira:

> I argued with her, but as one would argue with a *señora* [a lady], not like with someone my own age. One must respect a *señora*, she is already an elder. You must not say strong words. Maybe if I were to argue with her daughter we would really fight but with the *señora*? It's not possible, she is older. You have to use soft words, not strong ones. You have to know how to handle these things . . . if you are polite and have education; if you don't have education, you can say whatever you want.
>
> MT: What would happen if you spoke sternly with her?
>
> Flora: Well no, it's impolite. People who do that have no manners . . . no, you just can't do that. But she is pushing me to say anything to her [*a que le diga cualquier cosa*]. Because she's abusive, because she's older. She's older and she's abusive and that is why she is taunting me. I restrained what I said to her, I am holding it in [*yo me soportado*], to a *señora*, to an elder, the neighbors listening . . . what would they say to me? "Ay, that Flora is so bad-mannered/poorly raised [*¡malcriada!*]" Well no, I can't do that.
>
> MT: Did you feel sick at the time?

Flora: Yes, I had a strong headache, I felt like disappearing, I felt like just taking my stuff and leaving, going very far away. It's true.

Flora had a sense of social propriety and what would not be socially acceptable in her interactions with the elderly neighbor. She was afraid of criticism from her neighbors and that this conflict might cause problems with other neighbors as they "took sides." This, she feared, might potentially spread her conflicts more widely. She was also very conscious of the constraints that this placed on her and the ill effects these restraints had on her health. In an effort to avoid further conflict with the neighbor, Flora decided to give in and build her wall in the new location.

Throughout the period of construction on the house Flora experienced swelling in her legs and considerable discomfort. She sought out treatment with two doctors in Cochabamba (at a substantial expense) and an herbalist, but none was able to improve her condition. She asked me to accompany her to visit a ritualist, Don Miguel, who had ample experience with treating problems related to envy and sorcery. He was very devoted to Bombori and said he healed on the saint's behalf. Flora was diagnosed with several ailments, including arrebato, Pachamama, as well as other folk maladies.[6] Arrebato, as visited in previous chapters, emerges in the face of enduring anger. Pachamama is a folk illness that manifests when certain emotions are expressed in particular areas of the natural landscape. But of greater concern to Flora was the diagnosis the healer made of *envidia*. Flora looked visibly worried as she heard her diagnosis and asked what could be done. He recommended that her house and her daughter's house be ritually cleansed and "fenced" so no evil (*maldición*) would arrive anymore. They agreed upon a time for him to come to her house and the price for his services, which Flora unsuccessfully tried to negotiate.

After this meeting Flora returned to the market to work. As she reflected on Don Miguel's news, she became increasingly worried. Pondering on the issue of envy, she told me that she had noticed her sales had also been going down: "I am no longer selling the same amount . . . here people are evil [*mala*], here too there is envy." When I pointed out that perhaps everyone was having trouble because of the economic recession, she quickly pointed out, "It is affecting *me* more!" Since the construction had begun, she said neighbors and fellow market vendors had been envious of her good fortune. She would not, therefore, be surprised if someone was trying to do her harm.

In addition to the rituals performed at Flora's house, Mariana also asked Don Miguel to bless her new house and store. In addition to having the new house ritually "fenced," Mariana agreed to another ritual in which she was "re-baptized." She and her store were given new names, which she was not to disclose to anyone. She explained:

> That way, if someone wants to ensorcell me, it will not reach me—because they will hex Mariana and I will no longer go by the name of Mariana. And if they hex my store, that name will also be different. People will still call me by that name but neither I nor my store will have the same names anymore. Therefore any ill wishes will not reach me or my store.

Don Miguel thus developed a clever preventive and creative solution. Mariana was not yet as well established as her mother and so Don Miguel knew that Mariana would face difficulties as she tried to establish herself. She would certainly have to worry about the neighbor who was bound to lose some business as her store prospered. Her name, one's key reference in a social network, was changed privately so that witchcraft would not reach her. Flora in turn, continued her devotion to Bombori as well as to other saints. She had a small altar for him in her bedroom, and she lit candles and placed fresh flowers before his image each day.

The Escalation of the Conflict

A year to the day of the start of construction was Flora's fiftieth birthday. Her family and friends gathered in celebration for a meal, drinking and dancing to celebrate. Mariana had moved in to her new house with her sons, and her store was very profitable. After several hours of merrymaking the festivities were interrupted by the sound of breaking glass coming from the back of Mariana's house. Everyone was silent and glass shattering was heard two more times on the second floor. Mariana cautiously entered her side yard through the front store and saw that someone was hurling rocks over the wall which separated her house from the house of Doña Elvira. Two windows had been shattered. Flora called me to her side and said angrily, "You are a witness to what is happening here." Several other rocks were hurled, and Flora's eldest son went to the neighbor's door to confront the perpetrator, but no one answered his persistent knocking. Immediately, Flora went to the police station to see if they could stop the destruction. Both Mariana and Flora suspected that Rita, Doña Elvira's daughter, was responsible for the upheaval. Rita often tended the neighboring front store while her mother rested. Clearly their income had gone down with the competition from Mariana's store. The guard at the police station told Flora that no one could help because there had been a big fight in a neighboring village and only two officers were in Punata. Exasperated, Flora persisted with a bribe and the guard reluctantly came to the house to assess the damage. He told her to take pictures of the damage and to file a complaint the following day.

Throughout the night Flora's friends, compadres, and comadres came by to wish her a happy birthday and to offer her drinks of chicha. The guests tried to calm a distraught Flora and reassure her "they must be drunk, tomorrow everything will be straightened out." As the chicha continued to flow, Flora became more upset and began to cry. She came to my side and asked: "Why is this happening to me? What have I done for her to do this to me? What have I done? Who do I hurt? Didn't I work hard to build this house? Why doesn't she work hard too? Why have they hurled things at my house? I wish she would throw rocks at me but not at my house!" Mariana, seeing that her mother had had too much to drink, came to her side, gently placing her arms around her and escorting her home to put her to sleep.

The following day, at the break of dawn, Flora was preparing to leave for the market while Doña Elvira swept the front of her house. Since I had spent the night at Mariana's, I was drawn out of sleep by a heated argument between Flora and Doña Elvira. Speaking in Quechua, Flora asked Doña Elvira why her daughter Rita had smashed three of Mariana's windows hours earlier. Doña Elvira replied that Flora's two grandchildren regularly threw garbage over the wall and into her patio. Flora asked why she never complained and shouted that she had no right to break the windows of Mariana's brand new house. The argument escalated in volume and in intensity as they both vented their opinions and anger at each other in Quechua for several long minutes. Flora finally asked Doña Elvira: "Why don't you work? I built this house with my hard labor; its not my fault that you don't work." Doña Elvira's voice could be heard below Flora's, complaining about the children. Suddenly, Flora paused as if to collect her composure and switched to Spanish: "¡*Ya no eres mi mayor!*" "You are no longer my elder!" Doña Elvira replied in Quechua, "You keep your grandchildren from throwing garbage over this wall and into my patio!" "You are no longer my elder!" repeated Flora more forcefully. Don Agustín, another neighbor, came out of his house to appease the argument. "Let's take things calmly ladies," he said in Spanish. Flora turned her back to both of them and walked away.

This exchange reveals to us some very important issues regarding how Flora and Elvira had interacted up until that point. Flora had consistently sought to avoid conflict with her neighbor, but with this new physical affront to her house, Flora had lost her patience and temper. She reached her limit and publicly redefined her social relation to Elvira, which would allow her greater freedom (and social sanction) to express her emotions. Within the context of Punata, shouting "You are no longer my elder!" was a particularly strong warning. It was also a statement that revealed Flora's effort to reposition herself in relation to Doña Elvira. This was made possible by the fact that there was physical destruction of the house and that Flora felt that most neighbors would side with her and join in her dismay over the elderly neighbor's lack of respect for Flora's property.

The argument between Doña Elvira and Flora clearly represented a culmination of the quotidian stresses and conflicts that accumulated between them for more than a year. Flora, by publicly stating she would no longer treat Elvira in the same way, redefined their positions to one another. This new position granted Flora privileges to express her emotions. By the time I left Punata several months later, the conflict between the neighbors seemed to have subsided. They didn't talk to one another or get in each other's way. Flora felt that, in light of the final argument they had, if Elvira bothered them again she would no longer treat her with the same respect she once had. The broken windows were never repaired. Flora felt the neighbors should pay for the damages and continued to wait for a court order. Flora's health problems were still not completely resolved. She continued to try different treatments and hoped to find something that worked once and for all. The pain was not as bad as it had been in months past, but it had not disappeared either. When I asked what she was going to do next, she replied that she was not certain.

Several months after I was back in the United States I got a brief phone call from a friend who had gone to visit Flora and Mariana in Punata. Flora was much better, and the family was very hopeful that her health problems would soon be resolved. A healer had told them that she had a mild case of susto, fright, from an earthquake that happened before I had left, the epicenter of which was several miles away from Punata. Her ánimo had to be summoned once again through rituals. I recalled how frightened Flora was when the earthquake happened. She had moved her bed near the door to be able to run into the street during the aftershocks. She regularly had nightmares about a wall that would fall, crush her, and kill her. Negative dreams such as these are seen as *malagueros*, forecasters of bad fortune. When she had such dreams, however, she would do something a friend had recommended to her: "They say that you have to tell your dog your dreams and he takes it away. I tell my *Negrito*. I hold his little head in my hands and whisper to him my dream: 'I had such and such a dream . . . ' and the dog takes it away and nothing happens. Since dogs walk around everywhere, they take the bad things away and leave it somewhere." A detailed micro-examination of Flora's case allows us to see that she holds multiple interpretations and detects multiple origins for her ailments, and these are intrinsically related to details of her family and community relationships and personal history. These interpretations and origins speak to the emotions that emerged from the entanglement of social conflict, changing social roles, family strife, and on a larger scale to the discord that emerges by shifting social orders (such as changing relationships between generations and conflictive attitudes toward ambition and success). Flora's experience further reflects quotidian problems, conflicts, and disappointments and shows the relationship between fissures of sociality, emotions, and illness.

Flora's narrative, and her recollections of her conflicts particularly, highlight the negotiation inherent in the expression of emotions. If we look at Flora's conflict with her neighbor, her ability to voice her anger and frustration was constrained by the fact that her neighbor was older than Flora. To openly express her emotions would be considered extremely disrespectful and, as Flora pointed out, "impolite." She feared criticism and further conflicts with other members of the community, which, in turn, would continue to play out as a negative effect on her health. Initially, Flora made efforts to interact with Elvira as an "equal," as a property owner, but such interactions were not effective or accepted by Doña Elvira. It was only after the destructive demonstration of Elvira's resentment that Flora felt entitled to redefine her relationship to her elderly neighbor. Such an act would enable Flora to interact with Doña Elvira with greater freedom of expression. It is interesting to note that Flora redefined her relationship to Doña Elvira in Spanish, not in Quechua, the language in which the argument took place. This linguistic shift may be seen as a shift in the type of interaction possible between them: no longer as neighbors or community members but a more formal and official relationship. After the conflict the neighbors completely avoided contact and interaction with one another. What Flora created by shouting "You are no longer my elder!" however, was a social space to interact differently with Elvira or at the very least the threat to interact with her differently. Mariana also underwent a process of redefinition. Through the ritual conducted by Don Miguel, the boundaries of the "self" were shifted when she privately changed her name and thereby reduced her vulnerability to envy and sorcery. Through a ritualized "rebaptism" she was able to achieve a certain degree of tranquility and a freedom from the fear that community members would do her harm.

Flora's illnesses and symptoms were charged with social meaning. The community conflicts in which Flora found herself represented more than the immediate conflict over a wall or a disappointment in her neighbor. They represented community unease with her shifting social position and subjectivity and competing notions of what it meant to live a "virtuous life" (Hunt 1998, 299). A virtuous life to Flora meant being able to provide economic security for her family, education to her children, and a certain degree of social prosperity for herself in her community. This, in her view, was done through her hard work in the market and management of social relations. This became increasingly difficult, however, as envy toward her intensified in the market and among her immediate neighbors. Flora may never have found a clear "organic" basis to her ailments, but her symptoms clearly had weighty cultural and individual meaning (Farmer 1988). Flora is an upwardly mobile chola who was constantly being asked to be a godmother at weddings or a sponsor (*pasante*) at fiestas. She was in an economic situation that permitted her not only to build a house for her daughter but also to send her sons to study at institutes in the city. One of her sons had graduated as a dental technician (he helped make dental prosthesis), and she proudly referred to him as the "doctor" of the house. This clearly fueled envy toward her and her family: envy over their ability to increase their social status even in the face of economically hard times.

When I returned to Bolivia in 2006 with my husband and four-month-old daughter, Flora continued working hard and persisted in her efforts to maintain her prosperity. Two sons had migrated to Spain, one had opened an Internet shop in Punata, and Mariana's store was doing well. Envy continued to be a constant preoccupation for Flora, but in 2002 she began to sponsor a local fiesta for Tata Bombori in her home. She vowed to continue hosting the fiesta as long as she could. The annual fiesta to Tata Bombori also helped Flora perform her social ascent. It enabled her to amplify her compadrazgo networks as different community members were invited to help sponsor different aspects of the fiesta (Albro 2008). The festivities also sent a clear message to the community that Flora was a devout follower of Bombori and that through her faith she enjoyed his protection.

Religious devotion to Tata Bombori, either through the pilgrimage or through quotidian dedication, provided many market women with an avenue to negotiate the pressures that emerged from rising inequality and increased competition between vendors. While the desire for prosperity was alluring to all vendors, public displays of ambition were viewed with considerable ambivalence. The economic reforms had not benefited all market women in the same ways. Those who managed to succeed did so at significant social and emotional costs. Successful market women were paradoxically pulled in different directions as they were seduced by the promises made by the state, privileged their individual and immediate family interests, but also continued to rely on community ties, some members of which did not fare as well. The pilgrimage to Bombori provided a public avenue for pilgrims to be perceived as good and faithful Catholics, while more private devotion gave them a sense of reassurance as they sought to prevent the metastasis of envy and simultaneously obtain protection for their entrepreneurial activities.

5
Moving Sentiments
Emotions and Migration

Cochabambinos often joke that you can find one of their *llaqtamasis* (fellow Cochabambinos) just about anywhere in the world, and that when travel to the moon becomes more accessible, you will probably find them well adjusted there as well. There is a long history of emigration originating from the region of Cochabamba to other areas of the country as well as abroad (de la Torre 2006; Roman Arnez 2009). Indeed, one strategy families in Punata deployed to make ends meet during the economic uncertainty that characterized the late 1990s was migration. Throughout the 1990s the two key destinations for Punateños in search of employment were the Chapare region (see chapter 1) and Argentina.[1] Both men and women undertook seasonal migration to the Chapare, while males primarily undertook the voyage to Argentina to work in the construction industry. However, as the war on drugs became more aggressive and as Argentina began to face its own economic crisis due to the failure of its own neoliberal policies, migration to both places began to decline. Throughout my extended fieldwork, however, nearly everyone I interacted with had a husband, brother, cousin, or friend employed abroad.

When I returned to Punata in 2003 after a five-year absence, many things had changed. As I stepped off the bus from Cochabamba and walked onto the main square, I noticed several signs of prosperity. The plaza was completely renovated, and the Catholic Church was newly painted. Many dirt roads were now paved, as were several smaller plazas. The decentralization policies in full force while I did fieldwork in the late 1990s seemed to be bearing fruit, and public projects were being implemented and completed. Remittances from abroad were also visibly altering the local landscape as people built new Spanish-style villas. Empty, large stucco houses with balconies and decorative tiles flanked smaller adobe homes. When I visited the market, my initial optimistic impression was that it was thriving. There were many more sellers in the market than five years earlier. As I spoke to people, however, the same complaints were echoed over and over again. "There is no work," "everything is expensive," "the money doesn't run." I quickly realized that what I initially interpreted as a thriving market was, in fact, an engorgement of the informal economy that had swelled to accommodate the unemployed. Indeed, there were many more sellers in the market not because there was a demand for their products but because they could not find work elsewhere.

In 2003 people no longer spoke of relatives living in Argentina. Rather, more and more people I encountered told me they now had relatives in Spain. Commodities made possible by these new sources of income were readily visible. Children carried new cell phones, sent to them by their mothers so they could be easily reached. Parents purchased land with remittances sent

Figure 4. Remittance house

by their children so they could build homes in the future. Young men sported Barcelona soccer T-shirts and young women paraded the plaza with clothing their mothers may have sent them from abroad. There were different characteristics to this migratory flow. Whereas previously it had been primarily men who emigrated, now it was just as common for women to leave as it was for men. Women often left behind children under the care of a husband, grandparents, or other relatives. Furthermore, the distance and cost of traveling to and from Spain meant that migrants returned less frequently. Families could thus be separated without seeing each other for years at a time. Such separations had deep emotional costs for both those who remained in Bolivia and those who left; this circumstance also profoundly reshaped gender relations.

In this chapter I explore how talk about emotions is influenced by migration.[2] What happens when emotions "travel"? What new ways of feeling and modalities of interacting with others emerge in the process of migration? Is affect reconfigured by migration, and if so, what new form does it take? To answer these questions I focus on particular communication strategies deployed in the context of the migratory process: practices of silence, secrecy, and obfuscation. Nearly forty years ago anthropologist Keith Basso called for increased attention to practices of silence and why it may be deemed a culturally appropriate response in particular contexts among the Western Apache. Following Hymes (1964), Basso argued that in examining modes of communication, attention should not only be focused on the codes, channels, and expressions people enact but also on the instances in which people decide to refrain from verbal behavior (1970, 215). Keeping silent among the Western Apache was prevalent when interlocutors believed their relationship to others was ambiguous and/or unpredictable. Similarly, I examine practices of silence and nondisclosure to reveal how migration strained social relations and as a way to provide insights into how beliefs about emotions endured or became reconfigured in new contexts.

I consider performances of "not telling" from two angles. The first is a transnational one in which a migrant may conceal information from family members back home (and vice-versa). The second angle is viewed solely from the context of Spain, where migrants may hide information from other migrants. As I hope to show, the practices of not telling and of camouflaging experiences of suffering or success amount to forms of preventive medicine. In the transnational context, protecting loved ones from hardship stories was motivated by the desire to prevent them from getting sick from sorrow or preoccupation. When carried out in Spain, practices of nondisclosure and secrecy were active efforts to protect one's own health from the envy and bad wishes of others. To understand both of these situations requires an understanding of how emotions are constructed in Bolivia and reconstructed in Spain. What migrants and family members intimately tell one another—and, more important, what they hide—demonstrates the extent to which "traditional" health beliefs about illness and affect remain vibrant.

Emotions at Home, Emotions Abroad

While the scholarship on the experience of immigration is vast, fewer studies have examined how emotions are linked with transnational lifestyles and migration (Ewing 2005; Velayutham and Wise 2005). Wise and Chapman (2005) note a lack of attention to how affect intersects with the new experiences migrants have as they encounter cultural difference. If efforts to fill this gap are to be successful, however, I argue that it is equally important for scholars to comprehend a particular population's constructions of emotions "back home" as well as the bodily experiences of the emotions they have. In the case of Bolivian migrants, attention must be directed to the "traditional" healthcare practices in Bolivia, in which emotions have a direct effect on bodily well-being, and bodily injuries, in turn, can cause emotional distress.

As explored in the introduction, there have been several critiques to a constructivist approach to emotions. One additional challenge scholars of migratory flows interested in emotions face is how to deal with the notion of "context." Constructivism places great emphasis on the cultural "matrix" in which emotions manifest themselves, which makes it difficult to describe the experience of people who straddle multiple cultures (Ewing 2005, 226). Certainly, the contexts that define emotions and the power dynamics inherent in social relations that shape their expression change with the migratory experience; however, migrants (regardless of their legal status) do not *immediately* embrace or reject the discursive elements that shape expression in the host country, nor do they "forget" or privilege the local discourses from their own home countries. The sociocultural matrices that shape emotions are cast wider and are more complexly woven. Roger Rouse, discussing the circuits that migrants create as they negotiate their movement between places, emphasizes that they do not separate themselves from one national space and adopt another but rather they construct a new "community dispersed in a variety of places" (Rouse 1988, 1–2). The same occurs with migrants' emotional lives and expression. The "cultural context" relevant to Bolivia–Spain migrants is necessarily a transnational one. Thus, emotions in this transnational arena have "local" meanings, manifestations, and effects specific to each country as well as a recombined "local" meaning that makes sense only when embedded within the transnational cultural trajectory of the migrant life. As migrants settle into new places, they become adept at concurrently drawing from and negotiating different emotional geographies (Escandell and Tapias 2010).

Constructivism remains a viable approach to examine how emotions relate to the migratory experience, but it is greatly enriched by articulating it to notions of embodiment—the way people experience their bodies and bodily processes (Desjarlais 1992; Lock and Farquhar 2007; Turner 1994)—and to influences of transnational lifestyles (Vertovec 2004a, 2004b). A transnational framework clarifies how constructs of emotions articulate with migration by acknowledging that people draw from a "plurality of cultural codes and symbols that go beyond the nation-state and also multiple locations of 'home' that may exist not only geographically but ideologically and emotionally as well" (Wolf 2002, 257). This consideration of emotions abroad and at home has warranted taking what Vertovec calls a "bifocal" approach, a term used to describe how migrants' identities and emotional ties are simultaneously "here" and "there," resulting from time and space compression made possible by practices of transnational communication (Vertovec 2004b; see Portes 2003). Thus, how a migrant conceptualizes emotion is shaped not only by the "emotional baggage" with which he or she travels but also by the new moral systems, social rules, and contexts encountered through migration.

Before turning to the specific ways migrants and relatives communicate with each other and the way migrants in Spain communicate among themselves, I explore some of the characteristics of Bolivian emigration to Spain and a few of the challenges migrants face.

Bolivians in Spain

In the late 1990s Spain became a primary destination for Bolivian migrants in search of employment. Most emigrated with the intention of returning to Bolivia once enough money had been saved to open businesses, buy land, and/or build a house. The Spanish national statistical office (INE 2007) reported that in 2006 there were 140,740 Bolivians residing in Spain. Fifty-six percent of them were female. The Spanish embassy in Bolivia, however, estimated closer to 300,000 Bolivians resided in Spain, only 20 percent of them with legal residency and work permits (Bárbulo 2007).

Initially, this intercontinental migratory flow was stimulated by a combination of factors, including demands for cheap labor and economic growth in Spain, and the lack of good job opportunities in Bolivia (Izquierdo 1996; Solé and Parella 2003). Fluency in the common language between the countries further facilitated migrants' incorporation into the informal economy, generally in the agricultural and construction sectors for men and in domestic and care work for women. Women were often better paid and had more job security than men, frequently upsetting domestic gendered relations. Scholars in the field of migration and gender focusing on Southern Europe have explained these gendered economic opportunities as resulting from the feminization of the Spanish labor market (Solé and Parella 2003). Since the 1970s Spanish women have increasingly integrated the labor market, and their presence has triggered gender-role transformations within households, creating an increased need for domestic help and caretakers.

Since 2008 the stress migrants experienced in Spain increased significantly as a result of the global economic downturn. In Catalonia, where many interviews were carried out, unemployment rates reached 11.8 percent in the last quarter of 2008, compared with 6.6 percent a year earlier. The migrant population has been hit even harder, with unemployment rates reaching 20.2 percent among foreign workers. Among the migrant population, unemployment has been particularly high for males (22.2 percent) compared with females (17.4 percent). In 2007 unemployment rates for migrant workers were half what they were in 2008: 9.9 percent for male migrants and 13.7 percent for female migrants. These losses were most felt in the construction and agricultural sectors (Pajares 2009).

Bolivian females have suffered the consequence of the economic downturn far less than female migrants of other nationalities due to the large proportion of these workers occupying positions as domestic servants. Thirty-five percent of all regularized Bolivian workers in Catalonia were domestic servants, which was an occupation performed mainly by females. In spite of the economic crisis, demand for domestic service remained high, since care of the elderly and of children remained essential for dual-income Spanish families. From the perspective of these domestic workers, however, competition for their jobs has increased, as has the need for these women to maintain their jobs, particularly if their spouses or partners have become unemployed. Wages have also decreased considerably for domestic servants as competition for jobs has soared.

New visa requirements implemented in April 2007 created additional pressure for Bolivian workers in Spain. Prior to 2007, visas were not required for Bolivians, although they could be denied entry to the country at the border. While there was always an element of luck in crossing the border prior to this new regulation, migrants became increasingly concerned about whether or not they would be able to obtain a visa if they ever returned home and tried to reenter Spain. Many Bolivians already in Spain thus viewed their stay in the country as their "one chance" to succeed.

Many of the men and women interviewed were unprepared for the difficulties they encountered upon their arrival to Spain. Most had been persuaded to emigrate by family members and friends already abroad. During phone conversations, relatives in Spain made proclamations of the abundance of work available and the ease with which one could find work. They spoke of monthly salaries in Euros that were ten times the amount that could be earned in Bolivia. Upon arrival in Spain, however, many found it very difficult to establish themselves, and often the reality of their experiences did not match the promises of economic prosperity and opportunity portrayed. While some found work immediately, others often spent months in search of employment. Even those able to find work quickly were nonetheless frustrated by the small remittances they could send home. Migrants spent several months and sometimes years repaying debts accrued in order to travel to Spain.

"Don't Tell My Family": Secrecy as Preventive Practice

When immigrants communicated with their loved ones back home, they selectively disclosed information to key people in the household and seldom discussed with others the stress that accompanied unemployment, dwindling savings, and discrimination or health problems. Although conversations with family members could occur on an almost daily basis via cheap phone calls, the Internet, or webcams, the depth of information shared was closely self-monitored. Likewise, relatives in Bolivia refrained from telling those abroad of the hardships they faced.[3] An understanding of these silences and self-censorship warrants an appreciation of the importance emotions play in a person's well-being.

Joaquín, a shopkeeper in Bolivia, for example, recounted the story of how he and his wife decided she should emigrate to Spain. In 2000 Joaquín and Isabela were doing well financially. They owned four taxis, which they subcontracted to other drivers, collecting a handsome income each month. They also owned a small grocery stand with an adjacent restaurant where they served lunch and dinner. Joaquín and Isabela had two children, and that year, when their youngest child turned a year old, they decided to have a birthday celebration, inviting many members of the community, relatives, and compadres. They hired a band and splurged on food and drink. Joaquín recounts:

> At the time, I had the taxis, I had lots of work. When my daughter turned one we threw a big party, and a little while after the party I noticed that things started to go wrong. I started to lose money, I had to sell my taxis and everything was going badly. There was lots of envy. So my wife and I decided that she should go work in Spain to earn money so we could start over. She had a cousin there who told her there was lots of work. So she left for the Canary Islands. . . . She's suffering. . . . she misses our children. It's been so long—almost two years. She tells me "Sometimes I get sick, but I don't want to tell you, because I know you will also start to worry and get sick yourself." I also don't want to tell her anything that is going on here—if we get sick, the kids or I—because you can start to feel very bad there as well. I just about conceal everything so that she doesn't worry, so that she doesn't suffer, so that she doesn't feel so afflicted.

Similarly, Teresa, a domestic worker in Barcelona recounted how she kept information from her husband about her turbulent start in Spain.

> I've lost ten kilos since I've arrived in Spain. I don't sleep and have no appetite. Life here is very hard and we suffer a lot. But I can't tell my husband [back home]. If he saw me like this, he'd tell me to return immediately. . . . You don't want your family to know you are suffering, and they also don't want you to know what is going on back home to spare you more sorrow. I know, for example, that my father is ill, but they won't tell me anything so as to not preoccupy me. I live counting the days for when I can return home, to my husband, my family, and my girls.

When interviewing migrants and their family members, our conversations were often interrupted by requests such as: "Don't tell my mother," "Don't say anything to my sister," "Don't tell my family." Such remarks did not imply a lack of trust in relatives but rather a careful selection of those with whom they would share details of their adversities. A bifocal constructivist approach to emotions—that is, a consideration of the ramifications of the expression "here and there"—coupled with awareness of how emotions are embodied, help us understand these requests for nondisclosure. Migrants were mindful of the ill effects that sorrow, preoccupation, and pining could have on family members (often elderly parents and grandparents or people debilitated by illnesses) and were likely to censor what they told certain family members about their own health and suffering.

Lucía, a twenty-six-year-old who studied business administration in Bolivia, tearfully recounted the difficulties she faced as she tried to get established in Barcelona. "I walked up and down the streets of Barcelona looking for work. I wouldn't even take the metro so I wouldn't spend money." Lucía had a lot at stake in her search for work. Her family did not support her decision to leave for Spain, and she felt she needed to prove to them that she could succeed. Her father, a construction company owner, adamantly opposed her decision to emigrate and was concerned that community members would think he was unable to support his daughter. Not college educated himself, his ability to send his children to college was a source of pride for him. Based on his knowledge of other migrants' experiences in Spain, he knew Lucía would be working as a domestic worker, nanny, or caretaker for the elderly—occupations he saw as "beneath" those with a college education. Lucía, facing poor job prospects in Bolivia, felt emigration was the only route through which to obtain financial independence from her father. For several months Lucía and her father were not on speaking terms. Although close to her sisters, she did not want anyone to know she was struggling. Her sisters and parents complained in Bolivia: "She doesn't tell us anything. In Spain, there is no fraternity among Bolivians, but she doesn't let us know."

Indeed, it took more than five weeks for Lucía to find work. During this time she carefully monitored her spending and would eat only once a day. She feared that if her family knew the truth, they would pressure her to return home. She described instances of hardship, sexual harassment, and discrimination as an undocumented worker. In retelling these conflicts she repeatedly asked for my husband and me not to disclose these difficulties when we saw her family again. "So they don't worry," she added. In her search for work, she met several women who were even more desperate:

> Sometimes desperation leads you to do things that you wouldn't think yourself capable of. . . . There was a group of Bolivian women who used to go together each day to the employment agencies to find work. So, one day, two of them and I were seated waiting and a Spanish guy shows up and asks "Are you looking for work? I can give you work." I was very scared; what if he was a policeman or something? The other two women, however, talked to him. A few minutes later they came back and told me he offered them a job as prostitutes, that they would make really good money. . . . The two girls told me "If tomorrow we don't get work [from the agencies] we are going to go with him, because we no longer have anything to eat." Even if I had been without work for more time, I don't think I would have ended up doing that. I would have swallowed my pride and I would have preferred to ask my father for money than take that route.

Eventually, she found domestic work. Although the children, according to Lucía, were very disrespectful and spoiled, she had the tranquility of a steady income and a place to live. She was also able to find work on the weekends at a reception hall but quit within a short time.

> They paid us well but . . . the owner was a jerk. . . . He told me "I will give you a house to live in and will sign the forms for you to get papers but only if you start going out with me." He kept pestering me. He called me to his office to pay me my salary one day and he was giving me more than I earned. I told him "No, I am supposed to make 90 Euros per Saturday" and he was giving me an additional 200 Euros. He pushed the money back at me and said "This is for you—why don't you think about my offer this week? Anyone else would surely accept this." I never went back.

Lucía did not speak of these conflicts with her family. She was concerned her parents might fall ill from sorrow and preoccupation. One sister sensed the difficulties Lucía was facing and told us, "Tell her to come home. The sacrifices she is making are not worth it; the emotional costs of emigrating are too great to compensate for the little bit of money you can make."

Requests for secrecy and nondisclosure, catalyzed by the desire not to preoccupy family members, were interwoven into many narratives collected both in Spain and Bolivia. Most migrants did not have large networks of friends or acquaintances on which they could depend, and they lacked the social capital that could ease their stay abroad. Nonetheless, they hesitated to share their suffering with relatives openly. The same effort to protect loved ones from negative information by "not telling" was also visible in Bolivia. While most people suspected their loved ones in Spain withheld information, they engaged in similar practices. The distress of numerous interviewees in Bolivia was readily apparent as they actively sought to hide problems or health issues from relatives abroad.

As we sat in Rosa's chichería in Punata, for example, she lamented her daughter Soraya's lack of job opportunities in Bolivia and cried as she contemplated ways to lure her daughter back home. Soraya was an only child and Rosa missed her terribly. Although she was only forty-nine years old, Rosa suffered numerous health problems. She had been hospitalized twice since Soraya's departure and attributed her ailments (diagnosed by doctors as high blood pressure) to the sorrow she experienced as a result of her daughter's departure. When asked how Spaniards treated Soraya, Rosa replied:

> Ay! About that she never says anything. It's just that she doesn't want to tell me—because we suffer crying. Since she has left I have already been hospitalized. From suffering, from affliction. For a long time I suffered from high blood pressure. The doctors gave me pills to take every day so my pressure

would not go up—for when I thought of her. When she calls me to ask how I am, she tells me "Mami, you should continue to go to the hospital, you should get yourself checked out." But I don't tell her anything, so that she doesn't worry.

Rosa knew that Soraya concealed her own suffering and sorrow, and while this frustrated Rosa, she engaged in the very same practice. When I met Rosa, Soraya was concealing other important information from her mother. Upon leaving Rosa's house, our field assistant (Soraya's close friend) told us Soraya was four months pregnant but had not yet mustered the courage to tell her mother.

Among Bolivian families the stresses and hardship produced by migration were believed to be the triggers of illnesses among migrants themselves and/or their relatives back home. The link between emotions and health influenced how migrants administered and shared personal difficulties with relatives. Practices of nondisclosure and secrecy tangibly demonstrated the relationship between bodily and emotional health and were a concrete and ongoing linkage between people at opposite ends of the migratory chain. Controlling emotional expression—that is, carefully selecting what information to share with loved ones—was a tangible way of *managing* the ill effects that emotions could cause for their loved ones back home.

Secrecy, Envy, and the Care of the Self

While visiting a friend in Cochabamba, she told me the following story.[4]

> A farmer owned two baskets filled with mice intending to emigrate to advance themselves. The first basket was filled with mice from Santa Cruz[5] and the second basket carried mice from Cochabamba. The basket from Santa Cruz was tightly covered so the mice could not escape. The basket from Cochabamba was left uncovered and mice were free to climb in and out as they pleased. When a bystander asked the farmer why the second basket was not covered he replied: "it doesn't need to be covered, as soon as one mouse tries to get ahead, the ones below pull him back down."

Each time I retold this joke to Cochabambinos, it generated hearty laughter. Recent anthropological scholarship on joking suggests that such laughter reveals implicit knowledge about stereotypes, prejudices, and biases (Goldstein 2003). An understanding of this joke requires knowing the stereotypes that exist about people from different regions in Bolivia. Two common perceptions that exist about Cochabambinos are that they have an entrepreneurial spirit, and their failure to succeed is often due to competition and envy from fellow Cochabambinos.

Envy, as a discourse, was as equally pervasive in Spain as it was in Bolivia. Indeed, the fear of envy among Bolivians in Spain poignantly shaped the way they interacted with one another. When migrants told white lies or suppressed information from other migrants, the motivations behind such practices were different from active efforts to conceal information from relatives back home. At the heart of the apprehension about disclosing too much information to fellow Bolivians were concerns about the proliferation of envy and the possibility that the envious may resort to sorcery. Silence and concealment thus remained a form of "preventive health," but such practices were intended to protect the self rather than the health of loved ones.

How did envy, its relationship to sorcery, and fears of physical or economic harm "travel" across borders? In what ways was envy reconfigured, and how did it affect interactions between Bolivians in Spain? When social circumstances gave rise to envy, a migrant's behavioral responses included subtle efforts to quell its manifestations. Talk of envy in the context of migration provided a rich arena to observe the effects of global inequalities and how these inequalities were intimately experienced among community members. Furthermore, talk of envy grants insight on the precariousness of newly forged social networks and how ideas of reciprocity and collaboration were challenged by migration.

The Etiquette of Envy and Failing Sociality

Like gossip, envy (or, more precisely, the fear of being the object of envy) shapes social behavior and acts as a social regulator (Dreby 2009; Foster 1972; Van Vleet 2003). But while gossip tends to be a more public performance that seeks to share information, entertain, or act as a mechanism to influence members of a social network (Dreby 2009; Van Vleet 2003), envy (*envidia*) is rarely displayed or disclosed publicly (Foster 1972). Being the target of gossip can have negative consequences for an individual's reputation, but being the target of envy among Bolivians can seriously cripple an individual economically and/or physically.

Luise White (2000), in an analysis of vampire stories and gossip in colonial Africa, argues that understanding gossip requires understanding the social rules, values, and conflicts of a society. This is a fruitful approach to the study of envy as well. However, since social rules, values, and conflicts change with migration, it is useful to tease out the similarities and differences between how envy was spoken about in both Bolivia and Spain. I begin with an examination of the features of envy that remained the same in both countries. I then examine some of the societal and cultural pressures that shaped experiences of envy and explore how talk and expression of envy changed in the context of migration.

In both Bolivia and Spain, people would rarely admit to feeling envious themselves, although there was a lot of talk of how envious others are (see Van Vleet 2007). Envy was almost always spoken of in the third person; thus it was never in the eyes of the beholder. In part, this was due to the perception that being envious implied admission of social and/or economic inferiority and unsocial behavior (Taussig 1987). One envied what one physically or economically lacked. But this straightforward explanation for why envy emerges among Bolivians overlooks important "side effects" of envy. In the Cochabamba valley, talk of envy goes hand in hand with concerns about the potential of sorcery. Indeed, among intimates the relationship between witchcraft and envy is taken for granted and often left implicit. Fatima, a thirty-five-year-old mother of two, explained how envy operated in her hometown of Punata

> There is a lot of envy when one gets ahead, when you start to have material things. People—your neighbors—see and then they say: "Why do they have all that? They are doing well; I too will do the same." But there is envy in the whole world, right? It is very common. So what people here do is that they go straight to the *curandero* (healer), with their envy and they tell him "I want them to die," "I want them to get sick." . . . Black magic is the worst.

Thus, if the envy a person felt were great enough, he or she would be seen as capable of enlisting the services of a curandero to hex someone to cause bad luck, ill health, or, in extreme cases, death. The work of envy was subversive, insidious, and underhanded.

In more rural settings in Bolivia (areas from which most of the interviewees originated), people regularly discussed envy and sorcery when referring to conflicts between community members. Indeed, envy and sorcery were perceived as one of the inherent perils of sociality (compare with Ferguson 1999, 117). A person who was the target of envy may not necessarily have known who envied him or her, but a change in luck, health, or fortune could lead him or her to conclude that the work of envy and sorcery was at hand. This is what made it so powerful: a victim may or may not know whether he or she has been hexed, although upon reflecting on their own situations they may speculate reasons for why envy could be present. Regardless of whether a competitor was envious or not, the threat or fear of envy's presence was enough to cause a person to change his or her behavior toward others by acting more secretly or downplaying any success.

In Spain, the mere existence of inequality and undemocratic economic and social success was a vibrant breeding ground for envy. The discourses of envy and competition that circulated among Bolivians in Spain (who were often members of the same family or community back in Bolivia) were catalyzed by the constraints and opportunities posed by the receiving labor market (Hondagneu-Sotelo 1994; Fernandez-Kelley 1983; Menjívar 2002; Sassen 1984). Furthermore, the narratives of envy and competition, while shaped by adverse labor conditions, were also an intricate part of "traditional" discourses and folk constructions of illness and misfortune, and a reflection of rules of sociality in Bolivia (Crandon 1983; Crandon-Malamud 1991; Hammer 1997; Hawkins and Price 2001; Tapias 2006a, 2006b; Van Vleet 2003). As migrants traversed borders, they forged new social ties and developed new networks. These ties and networks, however, were strained by the hardships of migration and were not always very reliable. Indeed, throughout interviews envy was regularly evoked as people tried to explain conflicts with others and as they navigated between the pull they felt between meeting their responsibilities to the community of migrants and their desires to get ahead. However, as talk of envy traveled, it also took on new configurations. While the perception that envy was dangerous to a person's well-being was as prevalent in Spain as it was in Bolivia, explicit talk of sorcery was more camouflaged. Prior to exploring why this was so, a discussion of why envy flourished in Spain is warranted.

A person's purchasing power and material wealth; a good job and decent working conditions; the ability to save money and send remittances home; the ability to send children to college; legal working and residency papers—these are all things that could unravel feelings of envy in relatives and neighbors. Attaining these different forms of wealth, however, was always a challenge. Those who secured steady employment and regularly sent home remittances often accomplished such feats through considerable physical and emotional sacrifice. Nonetheless, those who succeeded were often seen (by less fortunate migrants) as being very ambitious—an attribute, as we have seen, viewed with great ambivalence among Bolivians. When a person was too ambitious, it implied that he or she had looked out more for personal gain than the well-being of the community, challenging "traditional" ideas of reciprocity.

The unpredictability of whether people will act in their own best interests or meet moral obligations to the collective good generated mistrust. In both

Bolivia and Spain, migrants and their family members and friends complained, "There is no fraternity among Bolivians"; "There is no trust [*confianza*]." This disillusionment was echoed by every migrant we interviewed, and each had a story about mistreatment from their *propios paisanos*, their very own countrymen, or even from family members or compadres. Often the very same relatives and friends who encouraged immigration ended up disappointing newly arrived migrants. Ironically, family members in Bolivia had peace of mind knowing their children, siblings, or spouses were migrating to a country where relatives and others would help them. The realities of migration, however, stressed these relationships, often to the point of dissolving them (Menjívar 1995; Napolitano Quayson 2005).

Alejandro, a twenty-three-year old who, at the time of our interview, was unemployed, explained, for example, how his cousin had failed him. The day before Alejandro's trip his cousin called him in Bolivia and told him to take a bus from the Madrid airport to the city where he was living.

> I was at the gateway of the world. It was the first time I had left Bolivia. I hailed a cab and went to the train station where I was to take a train to Lugo. I didn't know anything. I didn't know how to use the phone, I didn't know the European money, I was very scared.... My first job was to take care of some cattle. ... It was very cold there and I only lasted about a month. I told my cousin I wanted to leave and that I wanted to be paid for what I had done. He told me he was giving me room and board, so he didn't owe me anything. So I left.

Alejandro and his cousin were no longer on speaking terms. Maria, a caretaker of an elderly woman, tearfully recounted a similar story regarding her cousin: "She promised she would meet me [at the airport] and never did. I had no idea where to go or what to do; I didn't know anyone here. I didn't know the currency, I didn't know how to get around.... I was terrified—you have no idea how much I suffered." Dora, a twenty-eight-year-old janitor, complained of her sister-in-law's envy regarding Dora's ability to find work in Spain. "They made my life impossible; they told my husband that I was sleeping around and not coming home at night." Dora eventually moved out of their apartment because she realized they were overcharging her for rent.

Migrants talk of relatives who refused to share contacts in Spain, family members who became job brokers and kept a percentage of worker's salaries, or friends who spread rumors to tarnish a person's reputation: all such instances illustrate how migration altered the power relations and trust between family members and friends. In Bolivia, these relations may have been on a more equal footing, but in Spain, the newly arrived were very dependent on and often disappointed by their relatives. Because of the lack of trust in the available networks, migrants often feared that if they succeeded economically, they would be the target of envy, and this would dampen their success.

Don't Tell My Compañeras: Antidotes to Envy

In light of faulty social networks, migrants were careful with the information they disclosed to others. People did not freely share information about earnings, savings, remittances, purchases, or even how many jobs they had. In 2008, Teresa, the woman requesting we not tell her husband of her difficulties, also pleaded for us not to share information about her with her three roommates. Only hours earlier we had all shared a meal, and the three women appeared to be the best of friends. Teresa was keenly aware that her good fortune regarding employment was not the norm, and she was concerned her roommates would be envious. Unlike her roommates, Teresa came to Spain with work already lined up: a cousin who was returning to Bolivia "gave" her job to Teresa. "I arrived in Barcelona at 5:00 P.M. on a Wednesday and was working at 7:00 A.M. on Thursday." Eight months after her initial arrival, Teresa was working six days a week, cleaning seven households and the stairways of an apartment building. Teresa felt watched by her roommates, and they continuously asked how many jobs she had.

> It's just that there is a lot of *miramiento* [vigilance]. People are envious. I tell them I only clean four houses and that on the other days I go to an agency to look for work. If they knew how many jobs I had, they would say I was selfish and would envy me. I just want to make enough money to go back home to my three daughters. I cannot afford to lose any of my jobs.

Teresa felt the less information others had about her, the less vulnerable she was to their ill wishes. She was concerned others would view her as "selfish," implying that she had more than her fair share of jobs. Furthermore, unlike other immigrants, Teresa's economic situation in Bolivia was not precarious. Although a secretary by training, Teresa had not found secretarial work in Bolivia. Her husband, however, was a doctor in the public health system, and they owned a house in a nice neighborhood. Teresa justified her coming to Spain as an effort to make enough money to send her daughters to college. From the perspective of the social expectations migrants have, Teresa's request for privacy and concealment was well founded. She believed if others knew of her good fortune, she might be envied and would risk losing one of her jobs.

Teresa never voiced explicit concerns about sorcery—at least not in Spain. When interviewed in Bolivia two years earlier over a cup of tea, however, she talked extensively about the dangers of sorcery and how people regularly used the services of *yatiris* to harm others. She explained the types of rituals conducted by healers and the way people combined Western and traditional practices. When in Spain, I asked her whether she was concerned about sorcery with her roommates or whether she thought about securing the protection from a healer; she said no and looked at us as if she had never done so before. Her silence on the topic of sorcery took us by surprise, as we had extensive recollections of her detailed, recorded narrative on how prevalent sorcery was in her community. This silence, however, is as important as her extensive explanations in Bolivia, and it raises interesting issues concerning how envy traveled and the new guises it took in Spain.

Overall, talk of sorcery was indeed downplayed, even though talk of envy was even *more prevalent* in Spain than it was in Bolivia. Sorcery was not offered as an explanation for concerns about social relations until we explicitly raised the issue. Some claimed they no longer believed in such things; others, relieved we "understood" their concerns, expressed them, telling stories they had heard. Undoubtedly, there was more ambivalence about admitting beliefs about sorcery up front. This is not entirely surprising. In Bolivia, the closer one moves to more urban centers, the greater the ambivalence surrounding ideas of sorcery. Mestizos, evangelical Christians, and the upwardly mobile, for example, adamantly deny the existence of sorcery. In urban centers, people also feared being seen as backward or uneducated for holding such beliefs. Such concerns were even more prevalent in Spain, where beliefs in sorcery were considered "unmodern." Several interviewees spoke about how they were ridiculed by Spanish bosses or other acquaintances for holding traditional beliefs.

These concerns echo findings made by James Ferguson in the context of Zambia. While conducting fieldwork among retired copper miners contemplating returning to their natal villages from urban centers, Ferguson found initial reluctance to discuss the topic of witchcraft. While some expressed adamant disbelief in such things, a little prodding often led these very people to admit that witchcraft was one of the "obvious dangers of rural settlement" (Ferguson 1999, 117). Furthermore, Ferguson found that the terms "jealousy" and "witchcraft" were often used interchangeably and argued for analysis that took seriously the very material threats that were linked to witchcraft—threats not necessarily linked to the occult but manifested in other forms of violence, such as poisonings and beatings.

While talk of sorcery may have been less prevalent in Spain, what remained consistent was that envy could cause material and physical harm in one's life. The case of Marcela, to which I now turn, is illustrative of these concerns.

"You Have to Be Prudent": Guarding Marcela's Success

Marcela, a thirty-eight-year-old domestic worker, immigrated to Barcelona with her husband, Julio, in 2001. They were among the few migrants interviewed who had obtained legal residence and working papers. As a couple they had managed to save enough money to purchase a small apartment in Spain. When we spoke in 2008, they were renting the apartment to a Spaniard and using that income to make mortgage payments. Marcela and Julio rented another apartment for themselves, charging three other Bolivian couples rent for occupying the other bedrooms.[6] One such couple was Cesar and Monica. In the context of reflecting on the difficulties migrants faced in Spain, Marcela began to speak of ambition.

> MARCELA: There is a lot of ambition—for example, the couple we live with, Cesar and Monica, we are all friends, but you should see what he is doing. He doesn't have papers, yet he's been here a year and his wife two. He takes six young men to work with him. His boss gives him sixty Euros a day, per worker, but Cesar pays them each forty and keeps twenty for himself. I think that's terrible, and I've talked to his wife about it.
>
> JULIO: We know lots of people who are like that.
>
> MARCELA: I spoke to her because she is my friend—we went to school together. For example, I tell her, why don't you and your husband eat well? Your husband earns enough money. But no, there is ambition there.
>
> XAVIER: Are there any issues of envy among you all?
>
> MARCELA: Me towards her, no. As far as me towards her, no. We are doing well. But they have envy. They tell us, "you already have an apartment in Spain." But we got that through lots of sacrifice! And it costs us: that's why we need to deprive ourselves of lots of things. We always thought it would be a good investment, instead of throwing

money away in rent. But the possibility came up of renting the apartment to a Spanish guy and that covers our mortgage. In any case, if he leaves, then we will just move in there. So I think that is why they are envious. They see that we own the apartment and they envy that. We don't say anything to anyone, nothing, you have to be prudent. But somehow, they found out. I'm not sure how, but they think we are taking advantage of them. You have to be careful because some people pay money so that things go badly for you.

The tensions that emerged between these couples highlight how ambition was viewed negatively. Marcela and her husband criticize Cesar for taking advantage of other workers and making a profit off their hard work. Such is the extent of their ambition that Marcela even implied that Monica and Cesar don't "eat well." That is, they penny pinched even in essential needs to accumulate wealth. Not surprisingly, Cesar and Monica also see Marcela and Julio as ambitious and taking advantage of others. By having the lease in their name, Marcela and Julio were in control of how much rent they could charge their tenants. Marcela and Julio's success, as demonstrated by their ability to purchase another apartment, was viewed as being possible because they exploited others—in this case, their tenants. Although Monica and Cesar remained living in the apartment with them, the relationship between them was strained.

Ultimately, Marcela and Julio suspected that Cesar and Monica were envious, but they felt such envy was unjustified. Although Marcela admitted that they were "doing well," they viewed their success as fruit of their hard work and the sacrifices they made to get ahead (and probably their own version of penny pinching). Nonetheless, their success was tainted by the fear of being the object of envy and possibly the victim of sorcery. Marcela never accused Cesar and Monica of enlisting the services of a sorcerer, but she stated, "Some people pay money so that things go badly for you." In the face of these tensions, both couples guarded information from one another so as not to instigate further envy.

This case also reflects how relationships forged in Bolivia could change drastically with migration and how subjectivity was reconfigured in new ways. Marcela and Monica knew each other in Bolivia for many years, as they had been classmates since grammar school. In Punata they had shared similar backgrounds and lived close to one another. Both faced the lack of job opportunities prevalent in Bolivia during the late 1990s, and both emigrated in hopes of advancing themselves. Indeed, Marcela had encouraged

Monica to emigrate, stating that job opportunities in Spain were ample, and she promised to help Monica establish herself. As of 2008 both women had fared differently, and the inequalities that were emerging between them strained their relationship.

While the literature on immigration and transnationalism is replete with examples of seemingly harmonious migrant communities who offer assistance and solidarity to one another and to their home communities through hometown associations and networks of support (see, for example, James 2007; de la Garza and Hazan 2003; Shultz and Draper 2009) the narratives retold in Bolivia and Spain upset such images. While not downplaying the contributions such associations can make to sending communities and the way ethnic enclaves can provide essential assistance to compatriots (which might otherwise be lacking), the experiences of the Bolivians interviewed in Spain upset images solely based on cohesion and unity among migrants. As Portes and others have argued, migrants' social networks can be highly contested social resources (Portes and Sensenbrenner 1993). In some contexts people can develop independent social networks (Hondagneu-Sotelo 1994) embracing altruistic values and in-group solidarity (what Portes and Sensenbrenner call bounded solidarity [1993, 1324]); in others, social networks may actually stimulate greater intergroup competition, as was the case between these two couples. In the narratives heard, both extremes were visible within migrants' networks. The very same network that could aid and provide support could become erratic, exploitative, and abusive. On rare occasions, migrants formed tight communities with fellow Bolivians. It was more common, however, for a more cautious solidarity to emerge, one in which migrants utilized certain resources made available through social networks (contacts for work; rooms for rent) but also enacted a series of self-monitoring practices that helped keep certain information (earnings; plans to return to Bolivia; purchases) concealed from such networks. Portes notes that social networks in many ways can restrict individual freedoms, and such restrictions are one negative aspect of the social capital that networks provide (1993, 1340). Similarly, envy can be theorized as a negative outcome of social capital and can act as a subtle mechanism of social control among members of the same family and community.

* * *

Beginning in the 1990s and throughout the first decade of the new millennium, immigration to Spain has been one of the principal economic strategies that many Bolivians have relied upon to earn a better living and provide a better life for their loved ones. The emotional costs of migration, however, were often very high. Families were often separated for years at a time, and they were forced to forge new forms of intimacy among one another. The withholding of information from relatives in Bolivia and vice-versa was an act of love and concern. The withholding of information from fellow migrants in Spain was an act of self-care.

A culturally sensitive and bifocal examination of emotions, as applied to the case of Bolivians in Spain, yields insight into the ways emotions and their effects on sociality served as important community markers when the boundaries of such a community have been stretched transnationally. Beliefs and concerns about emotions such as sorrow, preoccupation, and envy continue to underpin the interactions migrants have with their family members and with fellow Bolivians in Spain. As one considers how migrants in Spain and relatives in Bolivia communicated with one another and how migrants in Spain communicated among themselves, it becomes apparent that the regularity and speed with which information is shared and the instability of newly forged social networks unravels new self-monitoring practices regarding their emotional lives. Migrants rely on silence, white lies, and nondisclosure to protect others and to give themselves a sense of security. This self-monitoring reflects "traditional" beliefs that physical pains unleash emotional harms and, vice-versa, that emotional harms can manifest themselves as physical pains. In transnational communication, contact through cheap phone calls and the Internet stimulated increased censorship in the (sometimes daily) conversations migrants had with family members. Thus, they told one another about their lives and distress but also mutually considered how their own suffering affected the emotional states of those from whom they were separated. The monitoring practices occurred on both ends of the migratory chain: migrants protected their loved ones from the suffering they were enduring and vice-versa.

Among migrants in Spain similar communication strategies emerged but for different reasons. The migrants interviewed often feared the proliferation of envy and the potential dangers it posed to one's employment and wellbeing. In Spain migrants never boasted about their success and emphasized the emotional and physical sacrifices they had to make to be where they were. Through appreciation of how emotions operated and were conceptualized in Bolivia, we can better understand migrants' self-monitoring practices in both arenas and the concerns migrants had about disclosing information about themselves to others.

Conclusion

On May 27, 1998, a few months prior to concluding my extended fieldwork and the day Bolivians observe Mother's Day, Flora, Mariana, Marta, Vera, and I were out celebrating at a local bar/restaurant. The large locale with a concrete dance floor regularly hosted celebrations such as these, as well as weddings, baptisms, and other festivities. As the party began, the celebration was attended overwhelmingly by women, mothers, daughters, sisters, daughters-in-law, and small children. The women were joking, happy and in a festive mood. They told stories, took turns dancing *cuecas* with one another, and shared chicha from large, colorful, plastic buckets. It was easy to get drunk quickly during these celebrations, and I learned from other market women to pace my drinking with frequent trips to the bathroom (which enabled me to skip a round or two of chicha sharing) and making hearty offerings to the Pachamama that grew more and more generous as the night progressed.

The deejay played a mix of *cuecas*, popular music, *cumbias*, and what is known as chicha music. Women of all ages danced together, some more animated than others. Mariana took me to the dance floor where I danced a *cueca*, a dance usually performed by couples who wave a white handkerchief over their heads as they "court" one another. The women teased me about how much better my dancing was compared to the previous year. Next to us, Flora danced with her eighty-nine-year-old mother who barely moved her feet as she gently swayed and waved the small lace handkerchief in her hand. As the song ended, Flora embraced her frail mother and affectionately kissed her on the cheek. "Gracias waway"—"Thank you my child [darling]," said her mother. Flora then told her eight-year-old grandson Guillermo to walk his great-grandmother home so she could retire for the evening.

We danced and drank for two or three more hours. While sitting around a small Formica table chatting, the deejay played another song by a popular Colombian band, and several women collectively let out a shriek of joy as the first notes were heard. Marta grabbed me by the hand and said: "*Vamos!*" "Let's go!" I finished the tutuma I had been drinking from, wiped my mouth, and we went to the dance floor. There was suddenly a swell of dancers on the floor, and the song seemed to be a favorite among the women dancing. They sang out loud to one another, some smiling, some swaying with their eyes closed as they danced together. I had heard this song hundreds of times on the radio, but it seemed like it was the first time I actually paid attention to the lyrics:

> *Los Caminos de la vida*
> *No son como yo pensaba*
> *Como los imaginaba*
> *No son como yo creia*

> *The roads of life*
> *Are not the way I thought they'd be*
> *As I imagined they would be*
> *Are not the way I believed them to be.*

The song laments the hardships of life and the disillusionment the singers feel when they encounter the sharp edges of life. As I looked around at all the people on the dance floor, Marta told me this was one of her favorite songs. I was not surprised, as the song spoke to elements of her own life story and echoed her struggles as she sought to manage her business and her disappointments. Through the toils of daily life in the market, Marta, and many of the women whose company I was in, were incessantly worried about their financial prospects, their conflictive relationship to other market vendors, and they had continuous concerns about envy as they tried to become more prosperous. Like Marta, the scores of women dancing and singing happily at the top of their lungs also seemed to find echoes of their own experiences in the lyrics. For that moment, however, the women I was with seemed to experience a temporary feeling of tranquility and happiness.

* * *

This book examines how Bolivian market and working class women experienced the social and economic changes engendered by a neoliberal agenda enacted throughout the 1990s. My lens focuses on how female inhabitants in Punata weathered the political and economic conditions and how their subjectivities were reshaped and reconfigured as they aspired to improve their lot in life. Neoliberalism is not just a set of policies enacted through governments; it also has moral dimensions that reconfigure people's relationship to the state, to fellow citizens, and to one's own body. Under neoliberalism, bodies are new sites of consumption, desire, and aspiration, which must contend with the social mores that piece together sociality. Neoliberalism, with its focus on individual responsibility and freedom, makes it easy to blame individuals for their social and emotional woes. Such blame ignores the material, political, and economic foundations of suffering. As the stories retold in this book reveal, it is easier to blame a mother for the poor quality of her breast milk than it is to address the domestic violence, unemployment, and threatened gender roles that exist within households, just as it is easier to blame a mother who can't control her emotions as the source of her infant's diarrhea.

My work also adds to the scholarship on emotions, embodiment, and social suffering in the Andes by focusing on the ways intimate narratives of market and working-class women are intrinsically linked to broader national and transnational political economic relationships. The life stories explored within these pages seek to provide a detailed analysis of the cultural and historical emplotment of emotions that shapes experiences of suffering as neoliberal policies and politics unfolded in Bolivia. In particular, I demonstrate how women actively sought to control their emotions to maintain their own physical and social well-being (or that of their infants) and how in the process they also negotiated, contested, or reproduced particular social and gendered hierarchies. How women express their emotions under myriad social and economic constraints provides insights not only into how distress was embodied but also into the ways women are able to "do gender" through their social interactions with others. Furthermore, as women navigated the politics of emotional expression, they also had to be vigilant about how others perceived their behaviors and how their embodied distress affected their ability to attain or maintain a state of tranquility. Through women's stories I seek to explore what neoliberalism "felt like," drawing upon their local knowledge of the body, emotions, and sociality as these interacted in dialogic relationship with political, juridical, and economic state structures.

As the twentieth century came to a close, popular unrest against the economic reforms steadily grew across the country. The protests against the privatization of water services, which eventually led to the "water wars" in 2000, followed by the gas wars in 2003, led to the eventual resignation of President Gonzalo Sánchez de Lozada and, in 2005, to the resignation of President Carlos Mesa, whose short tenure in office was marked by more than eight hundred popular protests nationwide (Dangl in Albro 2006). While these politicians tried to continue steering the nation along the turbulent tides of neoliberal promises, the tide of mounting popular dissatisfaction only grew exponentially. While the elites have tried to portray the protestors and activists as against democracy, the vision of democracy held by these participants demanded democracy on different terms: ones that did not primarily privilege the interests of multinational corporations and wealthy Bolivians (Albro 2006).

In December 2005, Evo Morales won 54 percent of the vote to the unease of the United States and other Western partners (Albro 2006; Kohl and Farthing 2009; Postero 2005). Morales rose to power on the shoulders of powerful social movements united in the belief that the neoliberal reforms were not in the best interests of the populace. While Morales repeatedly has asserted that he wanted to dismantle the neoliberal apparatus, reversing its effects on the country has proven challenging. While Morales, beginning in 2006, has increased social spending, the international financial institutions persevere in asserting that the country should resume the reforms begun in the 1990s to catalyze a "fuller integration into world markets (Shultz and Draper 2008, 74). Margheritis and Pereira (2007), however, discussing the loss of credibility of neoliberalism in Latin America, argue that governments overly privileged macroeconomic stability and GDP growth as an index of development. They suggest that visions for development need to be more holistic, and any claim to assist development must be mindful of "preserving the environment, the consolidation of democratic practices, the building up of transparent and accountable institutions, and the implementation of social policies to attain equity" (38).

When I returned to Punata in 2010, support for Morales was mixed. While some applauded his efforts to include more women in his cabinet and in local municipalities, others were wearier. Patricia, an avid Morales supporter, had numerous posters of him in her living room when I interviewed her in 2010. She asserted: "Many people said the 'Indian' could not rule. Well, look—he is ruling, he is thinking and he is reasoning. Evo has given more voice to women and enabled them to participate more in the political process. He is improving the situation so not only the wealthy gain, but everyone can have an opportunity to give their children a better life."

Claudia, the owner of a small grocery shop who worked from sunrise to 11 P.M. was not so sympathetic to his efforts. She was particularly critical of demands being made by multiple constituencies, which she viewed as "handouts":

> I agree that a pregnant woman and the elderly should get assistance, but I don't believe that if a person does not have land that we should just give it to them as a gift. If that is the case, I myself am going to start a new social movement and it's going to be called the *"Movimiento sin coches"*: the car-less movement, and maybe Evo will come and give me a brand new car! I believe people should work hard, they can't just be handed things to them. It's not right.

For others still, there was no difference from one politician to another: they were all corrupt, dishonest, and looking out for their own interests. As I have continued to conduct fieldwork throughout the years, it remains apparent that the health experiences of women and children are a productive site from which to examine the effects of the economic situation in Bolivia and the role precariousness played in reconfiguring social relations. In 2010, the last time I was in the field, the women I have now known for more than fifteen years continued to "suffer" from emotion-based illnesses. While those who have prospered or remained economically stable since my fieldwork continue to worry about envy and the watchful eyes of their neighbors, others who struggled to make ends meet attributed their ailment to their suffering, their sadness at the fragmentation of their families through migration, and the anxieties about nonprospering children in spite of the education their parents have tried to provide them with. By coupling an anthropology of affliction and its emphasis on the intersections of local beliefs about health and larger political and economic factors with an embodied and discursive approach to emotions, performed in particular ways under particular contexts, we can begin to understand how women in Punata experience different forms of distress.

The illnesses and symptoms that women suffer from give voice to larger issues of social suffering, conflict, and injustice. When unable to find a language of expression protesting their ethnic, economic, age, or gender marginality, people in silence speak through their bodies. The body and the ailments that affect it act as a vehicle to communicate to a person's social network, transgressions in idealized social codes that help grant purpose to people's lives. When women in Punata find themselves experiencing social and personal hardship, it is through talk of emotions, sociality, and distress that manifest themselves in the body that the "power to endure" (as Veena Das calls it) is lived.

Notes

Introduction

1. This section examines the underlying tenets of neoliberalism, but as Lind (2002) and Phillips (1998) point out, many of the objectives are not "new" but have been prevalent in Latin America under different guises as part of modernization efforts well before the 1980s.

2. I am grateful to the late Bill Kelleher for helpful discussion on the changes in subjectivity brought about by neoliberalism and for suggesting this term.

3. I thank one of the anonymous reviewers of this book for suggesting this analogy.

4. This was confirmed to me when I returned to the field in 2006 with my daughter Marina. People were not at all shy about commenting on (and/or criticizing) my caretaking practices if they thought these were out of the ordinary (like carrying my daughter in a sling rather than on my back, not swaddling her during her first months, or breastfeeding exclusively even though my daughter was already four months old).

5. Medical anthropologists have long held an interest in the way patients seek care from plural medical systems (Kleinman 1980; Janzen 1982; Crandon 1983).

6. A *casera* is the name used for a regular customer or vendor from whom items are purchased or sold daily. When a casera relationship is established, not only does the seller expect loyalty from a customer, but the buyer, as a casera, also expects to receive especially good products (a good cut of meat, for instance, with little bone in it), good service, and a generous *yapa*—a Quechua term meaning "to add." A yapa is essentially a bonus on top of what you purchase. For example, if you buy a kilo of tomatoes, your yapa may be a free bunch of parsley. (See also Seligmann 2004.)

Chapter 1. Neoliberalism on the Ground

1. In 1998 Punateños were given municipal water from 5:00 A.M. to 11:00 A.M. and from 2:00 P.M. to 5:00 P.M. daily. By 2010 they were receiving water all day.

2. Taxi-truffi's are vans used to transport between nine and fifteen passengers. Truffi is an embellished acronym for *Transporte Rápido Urbano* (Rapid Urban Transportation).

3. See recent scholarship, however, by Scarborough (2011) suggesting recent "de-linking" of dress from ethnic identity among market women in the city of Cochabamba.

4. One way campesinas were distinguished from the *vecinas* who wore polleras was by their less expensive garments.

5. In the past thirty years or so the religious landscape in Bolivia has been shifting as more people convert to evangelical and Protestant religions. This was also reflected in Punata, where many people have become Jehovah's Witnesses as well as members of Baptist, Methodist, and other churches. Evangelical Christians referred to themselves and to one another as *"hermanos/hermanas"* (brothers/sisters). Conversion to evangelical Christianity often means altering one's past behaviors and, in turn, becoming more critical of the behavior of non-Christians. Conversion in many cases has torn apart families and friendships. While my work was undertaken mostly with people who identified as Catholic, it is important to point out that evangelical identities in Punata are also present and flourishing.

Chapter 2. Physicality's Sociality and Sociality's Physicality

1. For alcohol consumption among men and health, see Clark 1989; Finerman 1989b; Larme 1998; and Low 1989.

Chapter 3. The Intergenerational Embodiment of Social Suffering

1. Studies on the cultural factors influencing breastfeeding have examined the obstacles to breastfeeding such as work demands; pressure from families or hospitals to supplement breastfeeding with formula; the sexualization of breasts and the associated shame of breastfeeding in public; and perceptions of insufficient milk syndrome (Dettwyler and Fishman 1992; Greiner, Van Esterick, and Latham 1981; Makhlouf and Castle 1997; Schmied and Lupton 2001; Van Esterick 2002; Zeitlyn and Rowshan 1997).

2. It is interesting to consider the comments Silvia's doctor made about her milk. Although I was not present when he praised the quality of her milk, his comments could be just as much a form of encouragement to continue breastfeeding as an assertion that her milk was better than another woman's (which is how she interpreted his comment).

3. For an in-depth examination of the gaps between biomedical breastfeeding recommendations and the knowledge Punateña mothers hold about nursing, see Tapias 2006a.

4. There exists an extensive literature on contextualizing different forms of violence among intimates and kin in the Andes. See, for example, Allen 1988; Canessa 2005; Harris 1994; Harvey 1994; and Van Vleet 2008.

5. Many scholars have examined notions of debilidad in the Andes, including Bastien 1987; Hammer 1997; Larme 1998; and Oths 1999.

6. Other firms include Multiactiva, Vial, Orcobol, Invanc, and Orbol. For an excellent analysis of the role of the inmobiliarias during the 1980s and 1990s and their eventual downfall, see the report issued by CEDOIN, "Inmobiliarias: La Estafa del Siglo," 1991.

Chapter 4. Anxious Ambitions and the Financing of Tranquility

1. From Quechua, meaning "to pass between us."

2. The ruda plant emits a strong and unpleasant odor that is said to ward off evil airs.

3. Brothers and sisters here referred not to biological siblings but rather to fellow Christians.

4. For an insightful class analysis of a similar ceremony that takes place during the fiesta of Urkupina in Quillaqollo, see Lagos (1993).

5. In fact, Flora helped two of her sons establish one of the first Internet shops in town. She purchased four computers for them so that they would not become indebted to a bank or have to pay interest.

6. Arrebato is an illness that emerges because of an accumulation of rage in one's system. Pachamama is an illness often characterized by swelling that emerges because the Earth Mother feels that she has been inadequately attended to, particularly when one begins a new construction project. Normally a series of $q'oas$ (ritual offerings) are made prior to construction, in which the Pachamama is asked for her blessings.

Chapter 5. Moving Sentiments

1. Other destinations included the United States and Israel.

2. In 2006, in collaboration with my husband Xavier Escandell, who is a sociologist, I began to undertake fieldwork in Spain. Our research strategy was to interview transnational families at both ends of the migratory chain. We defined transnational families as formed by at least two generations, originally from Bolivia, and which had one or more members residing in Spain and who engaged in at least weekly communication over the phone or Internet. We began by interviewing family members who remained in Bolivia and then followed up by tracking down their migrant relatives in either Barcelona, Madrid, or Bilbao. We undertook fieldwork for four consecutive summers and interviewed members of more than thirty families.

3. For a fuller examination of the type of information that migrants might disclose to family members, including information on illnesses that may require the help of a healer in Bolivia, see Escandell and Tapias 2010.

4. I thank Maria Esther Pozo for recounting this anecdote to me and for an engaging discussion on envy.

5. Santa Cruz, one of the principal cities in Bolivia, is located in the lowlands and is considered a "rival" of Cochabamba. Since the 1960s Santa Cruz has grown

steadily into the main production zone of the country and is a center of agribusiness and export enterprises attracting internal migrants from across the nation (Postero 2007).

6. Undocumented migrants are unable to hold leases in their names. Thus, upon obtaining legal residency papers many migrants leased an apartment and rented rooms out to boarders.

Glossary

abarcas: Sandals with soles made out of old tires.
abuelita/abuelito: Affectionate term for grandmother/grandfather.
aire: Interchangeably used with *embolio*, which in biomedical terms is the equivalent of a stroke.
ambicioso/ambiciosa: A person who is seen as having deep ambition.
ambulantes: Itinerant vendors.
ánimo: Soul.
anyi: Reciprocal aid.
api: Hot beverage made of white or purple corn.
arrebato: Folk illness often affecting infants, caused by the ingestion of a mother's emotions through breast milk. Arrebato can also affect adults.
avanzar: To advance oneself.
awayo: Colorful woven carrying cloth used to carry infants, produce, or any other items on one's back.
buñuelos: Fried sweet dough.
campesina/campesino: Peasant.
campo: Fields, a rural area.
caseras: Special client with whom market women have a long-lasting business relationship.
ch'alla: Offering to the Earth Mother.
chicha: Corn beer.
chichería: Corn beer hall.
chola/cholita: Ethnic term, usually marked by dress, for women.
cholos: Ethnic term for men.
comadre: Co-mother.
compadre: Co-father.

compadrazgo: Fictive kin tie.
confianza: Trust.
conocido: Someone well known.
cueca: Traditional dance.
cumbias; Music genre.
curandero: Healer.
de vestido: Someone who wears Western clothing.
débil: Someone who has debility.
debilidad: Debility.
desahogo: To release emotions.
embolio: A stroke, in biomedical terms; also believed to be caused by sorrow or anger.
empanada: A cheese pastry.
envidia: Envy.
forastero: A stranger, someone from afar.
fregada: A difficult person.
fuerza: Strength.
gente de bien: "Good people," a term used for middle and upper classes, usually not indigenous.
gente de las alturas: People from the highlands, with the connotation of "uncivilized."
gente decente: "Decent people," a term used interchangeably with "gente bien."
hechizo: Sorcery.
immobiliarias: Saving societies that promise lucrative returns on investments.
indio/india: Ethnic term that has derogatory connotations in Bolivia.
lari: Ethnic term indicating someone of indigenous decent who is poor and destitute.
leche gatona: Milk spoiled by a mother's emotions.
llanten: Herbal remedy.
lugares virgenes: Virgin places; places in the landscape where it is dangerous to feel strong emotions.
madrina: Godmother.
mala: Mean, malicious person.
malaguero: Forecaster or sign or premonition of bad fortune.
malcriada: Ill mannered.
mestiza/mestizo: Someone of mixed Spanish and indigenous ancestry.
miramiento: Neighborly vigilante, gossip.
mistura: Confetti.
mocochinchi: Beverage made from dehydrated peaches.
Pachamama: Mother Earth, as well as an ailment that causes swelling and hives.
padrino: Godfather.
paisanos: Fellow citizens.
pasanaku: Saving scheme conducted with people you trust.
pena: Sorrow.

pendón: A flag posted outside an establishment signaling the sale and availability of chicha.
plata, no corre plata: No financial stability; a depressed market.
pochongora: Herbal remedy.
pollera: Pleated skirt worn by cholas.
puesto fijo: Fixed market stand (for which one pays for rights to use).
qoqawi: Snack.
renegona: Mutable person.
reniego: To get angry, feel rage.
ruda: Herbal remedy.
salir adelante: Get ahead.
saqra hora: The Devil's hour; times during the day during which it is treacherous to express emotions.
sonqo nanay: Pained heart caused by excessive sorrow.
suero: Serum.
suerte: Luck, good fortune.
susto: Fright illness.
taquipayanaku: Songs with sexually explicit lyrics.
tienda: Small store selling food staples.
tirisya: Illness brought on by sorrow and by pining for a loved one.
tojorí: Porridge made with white corn.
truffi: Public transporation van (*Transporte Rapido Urbano*).
tutuma: Gourd that holds chicha.
vecinos: Neighbors.
viveres: Food staples such as flour, sugar, pasta, etc.
yapa: An added "little something" given to shoppers when they make a purchase in the market.
yatiri: Healer who can also engage in sorcery.

References

Abu-Lughod, Lila. 1993. *Writing Women's Worlds*. Berkeley: University of California Press.
Abu-Lughod, Lila, and Catherine A. Lutz. 1990. "Introduction: Emotion, Discourse, and the Politics of Everyday Life." In Lutz and Abu-Lughod 1990, 1–23.
Agadjanian, Victor. 2003. "Competition and Cooperation among Working Women in the Context of Structural Adjustment: The Case of Street Vendors in La Paz-El Alto, Bolivia." In Menjívar 2003, 262–88.
Alba, Juan Jose. 1989. "La tirisia: Una nueva interpretación psicoanalítica." *Busqueda* 1, no. 1: 31–54.
Albro, Robert. 2006. "The Culture of Democracy and Bolivia's Indigenous Movements." *Critique of Anthropology* 26, no. 4: 387–410.
———. 2008. "Fictive Feasting: Mixing and Parsing Bolivian Popular Sentiment." *Anthropology and Humanism* 25, no. 2: 142–57.
Allen, Catherine J. 1982. "Body and Soul in Quechua Thought." *Journal of Latin American Lore* 8, no. 2: 179–96.
———. 1988. *The Hold Life Has: Coca and Cultural Identity in an Andean Community*. Washington: Smithsonian Institution Press.
Álvarez, Gonzalo Chávez. 1996. "Diez años de reforma estructural: El redescubrimiento del estado." In *Aspectos sociales de diez años de ajuste*, edited by José Luis Exeni, 3–18. La Paz: ILDIS.
Antezana, Oscar C. 2000. Causas y efectos económicos de la coca en la Chapare Boliviano. Miami, Fla.: LASA.
Appadurai, A. 1990. "Topographies of Self: Praise and Emotion in Hindu India." In Lutz and Abu-Lughod 1990, 24–45.
Arze, Carlos, and Tom Kruse. 2004. "The Consequences of Neoliberal Reform." NACLA Report on the Americas, November–December, 23–28.
Asad, Talal. 1973. *Anthropology and the Colonial Encounter*. Ithaca, N.Y.: Ithaca Press.

Bárbulo, T. 2007. "Último vuelo sin visa para los bolivianos." *El País*, April 1.
Basso, Keith. 1970. "'To Give Up on Words': Silence in Western Apache Culture." *Southwestern Journal of Anthropology* 26, no. 3: 213–30.
Bastien, Joseph. 1985. "Qollahuaya-Andean Body Concepts: A Topographical-Hydraulic Model of Physiology." *American Anthropologist* 87, no. 3: 595–611.
———. 1987. *Healers of the Andes*. Salt Lake City: University of Utah Press.
Beatty, Andrew. 2005. "Emotions in the Field: What Are We Talking About?" *Royal Anthropology Institute* 11, no. 1: 17–37.
———. 2010. "How Did It Feel for You? Emotions, Narrative, and the Limits of Ethnography." *American Anthropologist* 112, no. 3: 430–43.
———. 2013. "Current Emotion Research in Anthropology: Reporting the Field." *Emotion Review*, 5, no. 4: 414–22.
Behar, Ruth, and Deborah Gordon, eds. 1992. *Women Writing Culture*. Berkeley, Calif.: University of California Press.
Biehl, João G., Byron Good, and Arthur Kleinman. 2007a. *Subjectivity: Ethnographic Investigations*. Ethnographic Studies in Subjectivity, vol. 7. Berkeley: University of California Press.
———. 2007b. "Introduction: Rethinking Subjectivity." In Biehl and Good 2007a, 1–24.
Biehl, João, and Amy Moran-Thomas. 2009. "Symptom: Subjectivities, Social Ills, Technologies." *Annual Review of Anthropology* 38:267–88.
Blum, Linda M. 1993. "Mothers, Babies, and Breastfeeding in Late Capitalist America: The Shifting Contexts of Feminist Theory." *Feminist Studies* 19, no. 2: 291–311.
Boehm, Deborah A. 2004. "Gender(ed) Migrations: Shifting Gender Subjectivities in a Transnational Mexican Community." Working Paper No. 100. Center for Comparative Immigration Studies, University of California at San Diego.
———. 2012. *Intimidate Migrations: Gender, Family and Illegality among Transnational Mexicans*. New York: New York University Press.
Boellstorff, Tom, and Johan Lindquist. 2004. "Bodies of Emotion: Rethinking Culture and Emotion through Southeast Asia." *Ethnos* 69, no. 4: 437–44.
Buechler, Hans, Judith-Maria Buechler, and Simone Buechler. 1998. "Financing Small-Scale Enterprises in Bolivia." In Phillips 1998, 83–108.
Butler, Judith. 1990. *Gender Trouble: Feminism and the Subversion of Identity*. New York: Routledge.
Canessa, Andrew. 2005a. "Introduction: Making the Nation on the Margins." In Canessa 2005b, 3–31.
———, ed. 2005b. *Natives Making Nation: Gender, Indigeneity, and the State in the Andes*. Tuscon: University of Arizona Press.
———. 2012. *Intimate Indigeneities: Race, Sex, and History in the Small Spaces of Andean Life*. Durham, N.C.: Duke University Press.
Carsten, Janet, ed. 2000. *Cultures of Relatedness: New Approaches to the Study of Kinship*. Cambridge: Cambridge University Press.

Cartwright, Elizabeth. 2007. "Bodily Remembering: Memory, Place, and Understanding Latino Folk Illnesses among the Amuzgos Indians of Oaxaca, Mexico." *Culture, Medicine, and Psychiatry* 31, no. 4: 527–45.
CEDOIN (Centro de Documentación e Información). 1991. *Inmobiliarias: La estafa del siglo*. CEDOIN: La Paz.
Census data. 1992. Census provincial de Putana, vol. 123.
Census data. 1992. Instituto Nacional de Estadística, Bolivia. Available at http://www.ine.gob.bo (accessed July 20, 2014).
Clark, Mari H. 1989. Nerva in a Greek Village: Idiom, Metaphor, Symptom or Disorder? In Davis and Low 1989a, xi–xv.
Classen, Constance. 1993. *Inca Cosmology and the Human Body*. Salt Lake City: University of Utah Press.
Clifford, James. 1983. "On Ethnographic Authority." *Representations* 2 (Spring): 118–46.
———. 1986. "Introduction: Partial Truths." In *Writing Culture: The Poetics and Politics of Ethnography*, edited by James Clifford and George E. Marcus, 1–26. Berkeley: University of California Press.
Comaroff, Jean, and John Comaroff, eds. 2001. *Millennial Capitalism and the Culture of Neoliberalism*. Durham, N.C.: Duke University Press.
Comaroff, John, and Jean Comaroff. 1999. "Occult Economies and the Violence of Abstraction: Notes from the South African Postcolony." *American Ethnologist* 26, no. 3: 279–301.
Conzelman, Caroline S., Coletta A. Youngers, Jim Shultz, Caitlin Esch, Leny Olivera, and Linda Farthing. 2008. "Coca: The Leaf at the Center of the War on Drugs." In Shultz and Draper 2008, 181–212.
Cotoi, Calin. 2011. "Neoliberalism: A Foucauldian Perspective." *International Review of Social Research* 1, no. 2: 109–24.
Crandon, L. 1983. Why Susto? *Ethnology* 22, no. 2: 153–68.
Crandon-Malamud, L. 1991. *From the Fat of Our Souls*. Berkeley: University of California Press.
Csordas, Thomas. 1990. "Embodiment as a Paradigm for Anthropology." *Ethos* 18, no. 1: 5–47.
———, ed. 1994. *Embodiment and Experience: The Existential Ground of Culture and Self*. Cambridge: Cambridge University Press.
Das, Veena. 1995. *Critical Events: An Anthropological Perspective on Contemporary India*. New York: Oxford University Press.
———. 1996. "Language and Body: Transactions in the Construction of Pain." *Daedalus* 125, no. 1: 67–91.
———. 2008. "Violence, Gender, and Subjectivity." *Annual Review of Anthropology* 37: 283–99.
Das, Veena, and Ranendra K. Das. 2007. "How the Body Speaks: Illness and the Lifeworld among the Urban Poor." In Biehl, Good, and Kleinman 2007a, 66–97.

Das, Veena, and Arthur Kleinman. 2000. "Introduction." In Das et al. 2000, 1–19.
Das, Veena, Arthur Kleinman, Mamphela Ramphele, and Pamela Reynolds. 2000. *Violence and Subjectivity*. Berkeley: University of California Press.
Davis, Dona L., and Setha Low, eds. 1989a. *Gender, Health, and Illness: The Case of Nerves*. Health Care for Women International. New York: Hemisphere.
———. 1989b. "Preface." In Davis and Low 1989a, xi–xv.
de Jong Joop T., and Reis Ria. 2010. "Kiyang-yang, a West-African Postwar Idiom of Distress." *Cultural and Medical Psychiatry* 34, no. 2: 301–21.
de la Cadena, Marisol. 1995. "'Women are More Indian': Ethnicity and Gender in a Community Near Cusco." In *Ethnicity, Markets and Migration in the Andes: At the Crossroads of History and Anthropology*, edited by Brooke Larsen and Olivia Harris, with Enrique Tandeter, 329–48. Durham, N.C.: Duke University Press.
———. 1996. "The Political Tensions of Representations and Misrepresentations: Intellectuals and Mestizas in Cusco (1919–1990)." *Journal of Latin American Anthropology* 2, no. 1: 112–47.
de la Garza, Rodolfo, and Myriam Hazan. 2003. *Looking Backward, Moving Forward: Mexican Organizations in the U.S. as Agents of Incorporation and Dissociation*. Claremont, Calif.: Tomás Rivera Policy Institute.
de la Torre, Leonardo. 2006. *No llores, prenda, pronto volvere: Migracion, movilidad social, herida familiar, y desarrollo*. La Paz: Fundacion PIEB.
Desjarlais, Robert R. 1992. *Body and Emotions: The Aesthetics of Illness and Healing in the Nepal Himalayas*. Philadelphia: University of Pennsylvania Press.
Dettwyler, Katherine, and Claudia Fishman. 1992. "Infant Feeding Practices and Growth." *Annual Review of Anthropology* 21:171–204.
Dreby, Joanna. 2009. "Gender and Transnational Gossip." *Qualitative Sociology* 32:33–52.
Dunk, Pamela. 1989. "Greek Women and Broken Nerves in Montreal." *Medical Anthropology* 11, no. 1: 29–45.
Ehlers, Tracy Bachrach. 1991. "Debunking Marianismo: Economic Vulnerability and Survival Strategies among Guatemalan Wives." *Ethnology* 30, no. 1: 1–14.
Escandell, Xavier, and Maria Tapias. 2010. "Transnational Lives, Travelling Emotions, and Idioms of Distress among Bolivian Migrants in Spain." *Journal of Ethnic and Migration Studies* 36, no. 3: 407–23.
Eustace, Nicole, Eugenia Lean, Julie Livingston, Jan Plamper, William M. Reddy, and Barbara H. Rosenwein. 2012. "ARH Conversation: The Historical Study of Emotions." *American Historical Review* 117, no. 5: 1487–531.
Ewing, Katherine Pratt. 2005. Immigrant Identities and Emotion. In *A Companion to Psychological Anthropology*, edited by Conerly Casey and Robert B. Edgerton, 225–40. Oxford: Blackwell.
Farmer, Paul. 1988. "Bad Blood, Spoiled Milk: Bodily Fluids as Moral Barometers in Rural Haiti." *American Ethnologist* 15, no. 1: 62–83.
———. 1996. "On Suffering and Structural Violence." *Daedalus* 125, no. 1: 261–83.

———. 2005. *Pathologies of Power*. Berkeley: University of California Press.
Farquhar, Judith, and Margaret Lock, eds. 2007. *Beyond the Body Proper: Reading the Anthropology of Material Life*. Durham, N.C.: Duke University Press.
Ferguson, James. 1999. *Expectations of Modernity: Myths and Meanings of Urban Life on the Zambian Copperbelt*. Berkeley: University of California Press.
———. 2006. *Global Shadows: Africa in the Neoliberal World Order*. Durham, N.C.: Duke University Press.
Fernandez-Kelly, Patricia M. 1983. *For We Are Sold, I and My People: Women and Industry in Mexico's Frontier*. Albany: State University of New York Press.
Finerman, Ruthbeth. 1989a. "The Burden of Responsibility: Duty, Depression, and *Nervios* in Andean Ecuador." In Davis and Low 1989a, 49–66.
———. 1989b. "Tracing Home-Based Health Care Change in an Andean Community." *Medical Anthropology Quarterly* 3, no. 2: 162–74.
Finkler, Kaja. 1994. *Women in Pain: Gender and Morbidity in Mexico*. Philadelphia: University of Pennsylvania Press.
Foster, George M. 1972. "The Anatomy of Envy: A Study of Symbolic Behavior." *Current Anthropology* 13, no. 2: 165–201.
———. 1981. "The Order of Discourse." In *Untying the Text: A Post-Structuralist Reader*, edited by Robert Young, 48–79. Boston: Routledge and Kegan Paul.
———. 1988. "Technologies of the Self." In *Technologies of the Self: A Seminar with Michel Foucault*, edited by Luther H. Martin, Huck Gutman, and Patrick Hutton, 16–49. Amherst: University of Massachusetts Press.
Franklin, Sarah, and Susan McKinnon, eds. 2001. *Relative Values: Reconfiguring Kinship Studies*. Durham, N.C.: Duke University Press.
Freeman, Carla. 2011. "Neoliberalism: Embodying and Affecting Neoliberalism." In *A Companion to Anthropology of the Body and Embodiment*, edited by Frances E. Maschia-Lees, 353–68. Chichester, U.K.: Wiley-Blackwell.
Garcia Argañarás, Fernando. 1997. "The Drug War at the Supply End: The Case of Bolivia." *Latin American Perspectives* 24, no. 5: 59–80.
Geertz, Clifford. 1973. *The Interpretation of Cultures*. New York: Basic.
Gill, Lesley. 2000. *Teetering on the Rim: Global Restructuring, Daily Life, and the Armed Retreat of the Bolivian State*. New York: Columbia University Press.
Glass-Coffin, Bonnie. 1992. "Discourse, Daño, and Healing in North Coastal Peru." In *Anthropological Approaches to the Study of Ethnomedicine*, edited by Mark Nichter, 33–57. Philadelphia: Gordon and Breach.
Godoy, Angelina Snodgrass. 2004. "When 'Justice' is Criminal: Lynchings in Contemporary Latin America." *Theory and Society* 33, no. 6: 621–51.
Goldstein, Daniel M. 2003. "'In Our Own Hands': Lynching, Justice, and the Law in Bolivia." *American Ethnologist* 30, no. 1: 22–43.
———. 2004. *The Spectacular City*. Durham, N.C.: Duke University Press.
———. 2005. "Flexible Justice: Neoliberal Violence and 'Self-Help' Security in Bolivia." *Critique of Anthropology* 25, no. 4: 389–411.

Goldstein, Daniel M., and Fatimah Williams Castro. 2006. "Creative Violence: How Marginal People Make News in Bolivia." *Journal of Latin American Anthropology* 11, no. 2: 380–407.

Goldstein, Donna. 2003. *Laughter Out of Place*. Berkeley: University of California Press.

Good, Byron J. 2004. "Rethinking 'Emotions' in Southeast Asia." *Ethnos* 69, no. 4: 529–33.

Greene, Alison C. 2001. "Working Girls, Cancun Style: Reconfiguring Private and Public Domains in Practice." *Anthropology of Work Review* 22, no. 3: 7–13.

Greenhouse, Carol J., ed. 2010. *Ethnographies of Neoliberalism*. Philadelphia: University of Pennsylvania Press.

Greenhouse, Carol J., Elizabeth Mertz, and Kay B. Warren, eds. 2002. *Ethnography in Unstable Places*. Durham, N.C.: Duke University Press.

Greiner, Ted, Penny Van Esterick, and Michael C. Latham. 1981. "The Insufficient Breast Milk Syndrome: An Alternative Explanation." *Medical Anthropology* 5, no. 2: 233–47.

Gutmann, Matthew C. 1996. *The Meanings of Macho: Being a Man in Mexico City*. Berkeley: University of California Press.

———. 1997. "Trafficking in Men: The Anthropology of Masculinity." *Annual Review of Anthropology* 26: 385–409.

Gutmann, Matthew C., and Mara Viveros Vigoya. 2004. "Masculinities in Latin America." In *Handbook of Studies on Men and Masculinities*, edited by Michael S. Kimmel, Jeff Hearn, and Robert W. Connell, 114–28. New York: Sage.

Hammer, P. 1997. "'To Be a Woman Is to Suffer': The Interplay of Illness, Emotion, and the Body in Quechua Women's Experiences." PhD diss., University of Illinois, Urbana-Champaign.

Harris, Olivia. 1994. "Condor and Bull: The Ambiguities of Masculinity of Northern Potosí." In *Sex and Violence: Issues in Representation and Experience*, edited by Penelope Harvey and Peter Gow, 40–64. New York: Routledge.

Harvey, David. 2005. *A Brief History of Neoliberalism*. Oxford: Oxford University Press.

Harvey, Penelope. 1991. "Drunken Speech and the Construction of Meaning: Bilingual Competence in the Southern Peruvian Andes." *Language in Society* 20:1–36.

———. 1994. "Domestic Violence in the Peruvian Andes." In *Sex and Violence: Issues in Representation and Experience*, edited by Penelope Harvey and Peter Gow, 66–89. New York: Routledge.

Hawkins, Kirstan, and Neil Price. 2001. "From International Policy to Local Reality: Women's Reproductive Health Strategies in El Alto, Bolivia." In *Managing Reproductive Life: Cross-Cultural Themes in Fertility and Sexuality*, edited by Soraya Tremayne, 52–70. New York: Berghahn.

Healey, Kevin. 1997. "The Coca-Cocaine Issue in Bolivia: A Political Resource for All Seasons." In *Coca, Cocaine, and the Bolivian Reality*, edited by Madeline Barbara Leons and Harry Sanabria, 227–42. Albany, N.Y.: SUNY Press.

Heller, Agnes. 2003. "Five Approaches to the Phenomenon of Shame." *Social Research* 70, no. 4: 1015–30.
Hochschild, Arlie Russell. 1983. *The Managed Heart: Commercialization of Human Feeling*. Berkeley: University of California Press.
Hondagneu-Sotelo, P. 1994. *Gendered Transitions: Mexican Experiences of Immigration*. Berkeley: University of California Press.
Honkasalo, Marja-Liisa. 2006. "Fragilities in Life and Death: Engaging in Uncertainty in Modern Society." *Health, Risk and Society* 8, no. 1: 27–41.
Hume, Lynne, and Jane Mulcock. 2004. "Introduction: Awkward Spaces, Productive Places." In *Anthropologists in the Field: Cases in Participant Observation*, edited by Lynne Hume and Jane Mulcock, xi–xxvi. New York: Columbia University Press.
Hunt, Linda M. 1998. "Moral Reasoning and the Meaning of Cancer: Causal Explanations of Oncologists and Patients in Southern Mexico." *Medical Anthropology Quarterly* 12, no. 3: 298–318.
Hymes, Dell. 1964. "Introduction: Towards Ethnographies of Communication." *American Anthropology* 66, no. 6: 1–34.
INE. 2007. *Demografía y población*.
Inhorn, Marcia, and Emily Wentzell. 2011. "Embodying Emergent Masculinities: Men Engaging with Reproductive and Sexual Health Technologies in the Middle East and Mexico." *American Ethnologist* 38, no. 4: 801–15.
Izquierdo, Antonio. 1996. La inmigración inesperada: La población extranjera en España (1991–1995). Madrid: Trotta.
James, Erica Caple. 2007. "Haitians in New York City: Transnationalism and Hometown Associations." *Anthropological Quarterly* 80, no. 1: 289–94.
Janzen, John. 1982. *The Quest for Therapy: Medical Pluralism in Lower Zaire*. Berkeley: University of California Press.
Jorgensen, Steen, Margaret Grosh, and Mark Schacter, eds. 1992. *Bolivia's Answer to Poverty, Economic Crisis and Adjustment: The Emergency Social Fund*. Washington, D.C.: World Bank.
Kaufman, Leslie, Swarna Deenadayalan, and Adam Karpati. 2010. "Breastfeeding Ambivalence among Low-Income African American and Puerto Rican Women in North and Central Brooklyn." *Maternal and Child Health Journal* 14, no. 5: 696–704.
Kitayama, Shinobo, and Hazel Rose Markus, eds. 1994. *Emotion and Culture*. Washington, D.C.: American Psychological Assoc.
Kleinman, Arthur. 1980. *Patients and Healers in the Context of Culture*. Berkeley: University of California Press.
———. 2000. "The Violences of Everyday Life: The Multiple Forms and Dynamics of Social Violence." In Das, Kleinman, Ramphele, and Reynolds 2000, 226–41.
Kleinman, Arthur, Veena Das, and Margaret Lock, eds. 1997. *Social Suffering*. Berkeley: University of California Press.
Klima, Alan. 2004. "Thai Love Thai: Financing Emotion in Post-Crash Thailand." *Ethnos* 69, no. 4: 445–64.

Kohl, Benjamin H., and Linda Farthing. 2006. *Impasse in Bolivia: Neoliberal Hegemony and Popular Resistance*. London: Zed.
———. 2009. "'Less than Fully Satisfactory Development Outcomes': International Financial Institutions and Social Unrest in Bolivia." *Latin American Perspectives* 36, no. 3: 59–78.
Krieger, Laurie. 1989. "Nerves and Psychosomatic Illness: The Case of Um Ramadan." In Davis and Low 1989a, xi–xv.
Lagos, Maria. 1993. "'We Have to Learn to Ask': Hegemony, Diverse Experiences, and Antagonistic Meanings in Bolivia." *American Ethnologist* 20, no. 1: 52–71.
———. 1994. *Autonomy and Power*. Philadelphia: University of Pennsylvania Press.
Lancaster, Roger N. 1992. *Life is Hard: Machismo, Danger, and the Intimacy of Power in Nicaragua*. Berkeley: University of California Press.
Larme, Ann. 1998. "Environment, Vulnerability, and Gender in Andean Ethnomedicine." *Social Science and Medicine* 47, no. 8: 1005–15.
Leinaweaver, Jessaca B. 2008. *The Circulation of Children: Kinship, Adoption, and Morality in Andean Peru*. Durham, N.C.: Duke University Press.
Léons, Madeline Barbara, and Harry Sanabria. 1997a. "Coca and Cocaine in Bolivia: Reality and Policy Illusion." In Léons and Sanabria 1997b, 1–46.
Léons, Madeline Barbara, and Harry Sanabria, eds. 1997b. *Coca, Cocaine, and the Bolivian Reality*. Albany: State University of New York Press.
Lind, Amy. 2002. "Making Feminist Sense of Neoliberalism: The Institutionalization of Women's Struggles for Survival in Ecuador and Bolivia." *Journal of Developing Societies* 18, no. 2/3: 228–58.
———. 2003. Making Feminist Sense of Neoliberalism: The Institutionalization of Women's Struggles for Survival in Ecuador and Bolivia. In Menjivar 2003, 231–61.
Lock, Margaret. 1993. *Encounters with Aging*. Berkeley: University of California Press.
Lock, Margaret, and Judith Farquhar, eds. 2007. *Beyond the Body Proper: Reading the Anthropology of Material Life*. Durham, N.C.: Duke University Press.
Low, Setha M. 1985. "Culturally Interpreted Symptoms or Culture-Bound Syndromes: A Cross-Cultural Review of Nerves." *Social Science and Medicine* 21, no. 2: 187–96.
———. 1989. "Gender, Emotions, and *Nervios* in Urban Guatemala." *Health Care for Women International* 10, no. 1–3: 115–40.
Lutz, Catherine. 1986. "Emotion, Thought, and Estrangement: Emotion as a Cultural Category." *Cultural Anthropology* 1, no. 3: 287–309.
———. 1988. *Unnatural Emotions: Everyday Sentiments on a Micronesian Atoll and Their Challenge to Western Theory*. Chicago: University of Chicago Press.
———. 1990. "Engendered Emotions: Gender, Power, and the Rhetoric of Emotional Control in American Discourse." In Lutz and Abu-Lughod 1990, 69–91.
Lutz, Catherine, and Lila Abu-Lughod, eds. 1990. *Language and the Politics of Emotions*. Cambridge: Cambridge University Press.
Lutz, Catherine, and Geoffrey M. White. 1986. "The Anthropology of Emotions." *Annual Review of Anthropology* 15:436.

Lyon, Margot L., and Jack M. Barbalet. 1994. "Society's Body: Emotion and the 'Somatization' of Social Theory." In Csordas 1994, 48–66.
Maher, Vanessa, ed. 1992. *The Anthropology of Breast-Feeding: Natural Law or Social Construct*. Cross-Cultural Perspectives on Women. Oxford: Berg.
Makhlouf, Carla, and Sarah Castle. 1997. "Back to Nature? Historical and Cross-Cultural Perspectives on Barriers to Optimal Breast-Feeding." *Medical Anthropology* 17:39–63.
Margheritis, Ann, and Anthony Pereira. 2007. "The Neoliberal Turn in Latin America: The Cycle of Ideas and the Search for an Alternative." *Latin American Perspectives* 34, no. 3: 25–48.
Martin, Emily. 1987. *The Woman in the Body*. Boston: Beacon.
Maschia-Lees, Frances. E. 2011. *A Companion to the Anthropology of the Body and Embodiment*. Wiley-Blackwell.
Masseroni, Susana, and Susana Sauane. 2003. "Psychic and Somatic Vulnerability among Professional Women in Argentina as a Result of the Precarization of Labor Linked during the Socioeconomic Crisis." In Menjívar 2003, 61–83.
Maynes, Mary Jo, Jennifer L. Pierce, and Barbara Laslett. 2008. *Telling Stories: The Use of Personal Narratives in the Social Sciences and History*. Ithaca, N.Y.: Cornell University Press.
McNay, Lois. 2008. "The Trouble with Recognition: Subjectivity, Suffering and Agency." *Sociological Theory* 26, no. 3: 271–96.
Menjívar, Cecilia. 1995. "Kinship Networks among Immigrants: Lessons from a Qualitative Comparative Approach." *International Journal of Comparative Sociology* 36, no. 1–2: 219–33.
———. 2002. "Introduction." In Menjívar 2003, 1–10.
———. 2003. *Through the Eyes of Women: Gender, Social Networks, Family and Structural Change in Latin American and the Caribbean*. International Studies in Social Science. Ontario: de Sitter.
Miles, Ann. 1998. "Women's Bodies, Women's Selves: Illness Narratives and the 'Andean' Body." *Body and Society* 4, no. 3: 1–19.
———. 2003. "Healers as Entrepreneurs: Constructing an Image of Legitimized Potency in Urban Ecuador." In *Medical Pluralism in the Andes*, edited by Joan D. Koss-Chioino, Thomas Leatherman, and Christine Greenway, 107–28. New York: Routledge.
Mills, Mary Beth. 1997. "Contesting the Margins of Modernity: Women, Migration, and Consumption in Thailand." *American Enthnologist* 24, no. 1: 37–61.
Moser, Caroline. 1993. "Adjustment from Below: Low Income Women, Time and the Triple Role in Guayaquil, Ecuador." In *Viva! Women and Popular Protest in Latin America*, International Studies of Women and Place, edited by Sarah Radcliffe and Sallie Westwood, 173–96. London: Routledge.
Mull, Dorothy. 1992. "Mother's Milk and Pseudoscientific Breastmilk Testing in Pakistan." *Social Science and Medicine* 34, no. 11: 1277–90.

Napolitano-Quayson, Valentina. 2005. "Social Suffering and Embodied States of Male Transnational Migrancy in San Francisco, California." *Identities* 12, no. 2: 335–62.

Narayan, Kirin. 1993. "How Native is the 'Native' Anthropologist?" *American Anthropologist* 95, no. 3: 671–86.

Nelson, Diane. 2009. "Mayan Ponzi: A Contagion of Hope, a Made-off with Your Money." Available at http://hemi.nyu.edu/hemi/es/e-misferica-61/nelson (accessed July 20, 2014).

Ong, Aihwa. 1991. "The Gender and Labor Politics of Postmodernity." *Annual Review of Anthropology* 20:279–309.

———. 2006. *Neoliberalism as Exception: Mutations in Citizenship and Sovereignty*. Durham, N.C.: Duke University Press.

Orr, David M. 2013. "'Now He Walks and Walks, As If He Didn't Have a Home Where He Could Eat': Food, Healing, and Hunger in Quechua Narratives of Madness. *Culture, Medicine, and Psychiatry* 37(4): 694–710.

Oths, Katherine. 1999. "*Debilidad*: A Biocultural Assessment of an Embodied Andean Illness." *Medical Anthropology Quarterly* 13, no. 3: 286–315.

Padilla, Mark B., Jennifer S. Hirsch, Miguel Muñoz-Laboy, Robert E. Sember, and Richard G. Parker, eds. 2008. *Love and Globalization: Transformations of Intimacy in the Contemporary World*. Nashville, Tenn.: Vanderbilt University Press.

Painter, Michael D. 1998. "Economic Development and the Origins of the Bolivian Cocaine Industry." In Phillips 1998, 29–50.

Pajares, M. 2009. "La inserció laboral de la població immigrada: L'estat de la immigració a Catalunya." 1–27. Barcelona: Fundació Jaume Bofill. Available at http://www.fbofill.cat/intra/fbofill/documents/INFORME_insecio_laboral_immigrants.pkfckward.pdf (accessed August 30, 2014).

Parson, Nia. 2010. "Transformative Ties: Gendered Violence, Forms of Recovery, and Shifting Subjectivities in Chile." *Medical Anthropology Quarterly* 24, no. 1: 64–84.

———. 2013. *Traumatic States: Gendered Violence, Suffering and Care in Chile*. Nashville, Tenn.: Vanderbilt University Press.

Paulson, Susan. 1996. "Familias que no 'conyugan' e identidades que no conjugan: La vida en Mizque desafía nuestras categorias." In *Ser mujer indígena, chola o birlocha en la Bolivia postcolonial de los años 90*, edited by Silvia Rivera Cusicanqui, 85–154. La Paz: Ministerio de Desarrollo Humano.

Pereira, Rodney M. 1996. "Los indicadores sociales y los efectos de las politicas de ajuste." In *Aspectos sociales de diez años de ajuste*, edited by José Luis Exeni, 37–44. La Paz: ILDIS.

Petryna, Adriana. 2002. *Life Exposed: Biological Citizens after Chernobyl*. Princeton, N.J.: Princeton University Press.

Phillips, Lynne. 1998. *The Third Wave of Modernization in Latin America: Cultural Perspectives on Neoliberalism*. Jaguar Books on Latin America, vol. 16. Wilmington, Del.: Scholarly Resources.

Portes, Alejandro. 2003. "Conclusion: Theoretical Convergencies and Empirical Evidence in the Study of Immigrant Transnationalism." *International Migration Review* 37, no. 3: 874–92.
Portes, Alejandro, and Julia Sensenbrenner. 1993. "Embeddedness and Immigration: Notes on the Social Determinants of Economic Action." *American Journal of Sociology* 98: 1320–50.
Postero, Nancy Grey. 2005. "Indigenous Responses to Neoliberalism: A Look at the Bolivian Uprising of 2003." *PoLAR: Political and Legal Anthropology Review* 28, no. 1: 73–92.
———. 2007. *Now We Are Citizens: Indigenous Politics in Postmulticultural Bolivia.* Stanford, Calif.: Stanford University Press.
Pribilsky, Jason. 2001. "Nervios and 'Modern' Childhood: Migration and Changing Contexts of Child Life in the Ecuadorian Andes." *Childhood: A Global Journal of Child Research* 8, no. 2: 251–73.
———. 2004. "'Aprendemos a convivir': Conjugal Relations, Co-parenting, and Family Life among Ecuadorian Transnational Migrants in New York and the Ecuadorian Andes." *Global Networks* 4, no. 3: 313–34.
———. 2007. *La Chulla Vida: Gender, Migration and the Family in Andean Ecuador and New York City.* Syracuse N.Y.: Syracuse University Press.
Rasnake, Roger. 1988. *Domination and Cultural Resistance: Authority and Power among an Andean People.* Durham, N.C.: Duke University Press.
Rebhun, Linda A. 1993. "Nerves and Emotional Play in Northeast Brazil." *Medical Anthropology Quarterly* 7, no. 2: 131–51.
———. 1994. "Swallowing Frogs: Anger and Illness in Northeast Brazil." *Medical Anthropology Quarterly* 8, no. 4: 360–82.
———. 1999. *The Heart is Unknown Country: Love in the Changing Economy of Northeast Brazil.* Stanford: Stanford University Press.
Reddy, W. M. 1999. "Emotional Liberty: Politics and History in the Anthropology of Emotions." *Cultural Anthropology* 14, no. 2: 256–88.
Richman, Karen. 2005. *Migration and Vodou.* Gainesville: University Press of Florida.
Rodríguez, Gustavo, and Humberto Solares. 1990. *Sociedad oligárquica, chicha y cultura popular.* Cochabamba, Bolivia: Serrano.
Roman Arnez, Olivia. 2009. *Migracion y ciudadania en Bolivia en el context Latinoamericano.* Cochabamba, Bolivia: Centro de Estudios Superiores Universitarios (CESU).
Rosaldo, Michelle. 1980. *Knowledge and Passion: Ilongot Notions of Self and Social Life.* Cambridge: Cambridge University Press.
———. 1984. "Toward an Anthropology of Self and Feeling." In *Culture Theory: Essays on Mind, Self, and Emotion,* edited by Richard A. Shweder and Robert A. LeVine, 137–57. Cambridge: Cambridge University Press.
Rosenwein, Barbara H. 2002. "Worrying about Emotions in History." *American Historical Review* 107, no. 3: 821–45.

Rouse, Roger. 1988. "Mexicano, chicano, pocho: La migracíon mexicana y el espacio social del postmodernismo. In "Página Uno," supplement to *Unomasuno*, December 31, 1988, 1- 2.

Rubel, Arthur. 1984. *Susto: A Folk Illness*. Berkeley: University of California Press.

Sanabria, Harry. 1993. *The Coca Boom and Rural Social Change in Bolivia*. Ann Arbor: University of Michigan Press.

Sassen, Saskia. 1984. "Notes on the Incorporation of Third World Women into Wage Labour through Offshore Production." *International Migration Review* 18, no. 4: 1144–67.

Scarborough, Isabel. 2011. "Crafting Bolivia's Urban Middle Class: Informal Market Women and the Role of Identity Politics." Paper presented at the American Anthropological Association Annual Meetings, Montreal, Canada, November 18.

Schacter, Mark, Margaret Grosh, and Steen Jorgensten. 1992. "What, Why, How? A Primer on ESF." In Jorgensen, Grosh, and Schacter 1992.

Scheper-Hughes, Nancy. 1985. "Culture, Scarcity, and Maternal Thinking: Maternal Detachment and Infant Survival in a Brazilian Shantytown." *Ethos* 13, no. 4: 291–317.

———. 1992a. *Death without Weeping*. Berkeley: University of California Press.

———. 1992b. "Hungry Bodies, Medicine, and the State: Toward a Critical Psychological Anthropology." In *New Directions in Psychological Anthropology*, edited by Theodore Schwartz, Geoffrey M. White and Catherine Lutz, 221–50. Cambridge: Cambridge University Press.

———. 1995. "The Primacy of the Ethical: Propositions for a Militant Anthropology." *Current Anthropology* 36:409–40.

Scheper-Hughes, Nancy, and Margaret Lock. 1987. "The Mindful Body: A Prolegomenon to Future Work in Medical Anthropology." *Medical Anthropology Quarterly* 1, no. 1: 6–41.

Schmied, Virginia, and Deborah Lupton. 2001. "Blurring the Boundaries: Breast-Feeding, and Maternal Subjectivity." *Sociology of Health and Illness* 23, no. 2: 234–50.

Secretaria Nacional de Salud. 1996. "Analysis y Evaluación: Datos de Salud; Punata Cochabamba." Proyecto de Salud Pública Boliviano Alemán. Distrito II Valle Alto.

Seligmann, Linda J. 1989. "To Be In Between: The Cholas as Market Women." *Society for Comparative Study of Society and History* 31, no. 4: 694–721.

———. 1998. "Survival Politics and the Movements of Market Women in Peru in the Age of Neoliberalism." In Phillips 1998, 65–82.

———. 2004. *Peruvian Street Lives: Culture, Power, and Economy among Market Women of Cuzco*. Urbana: University of Illinois Press.

Shultz, Jim, and Melissa Draper. 2009. *Dignity and Defiance: Stories from Bolivia's Challenge to Globalization*. Berkeley: University of California Press.

Sikkink, Lynn. 2001. "Home Sweet Market Stand: Work, Gender, and Getting Ahead among Bolivian Traditional Medicine Vendors. *Anthropology of Work Review* 22, no. 3: 1–6.

Solé, C., and S. Parella. 2003. "The Labour Market and Racial Discrimination in Spain." *Journal of Ethnic and Migration Studies* 29, no. 1: 121–40.

Spedding, Alison L. 1989. "Coca Eradication: A Remedy for Independence? (with a Postscript)." *Anthropology Today* 5, no. 5.
Sultana, Farhana. 2011. "Suffering for Water, Suffering from Water: Emotional Geographies of Resource Access, Control, and Conflict." *Geoforum* 42, no. 2: 163–72.
Swaney, Deanna. 1996. *Lonely Planet—Bolivia: A Travel Survival Kit*. 3rd ed. Oakland: Lonely Planet.
Tapias, Maria. 2006a. "Always Ready and Always Clean? Competing Discourses of Breast-Feeding, Infant Illness, and the Politics of Mother-Blame in Bolivia." *Body and Society* 12, no. 2: 83–108.
———. 2006b. "Emotions and the Intergenerational Embodiment of Social Suffering in Rural Bolivia." *Medical Anthropology Quarterly* 20, no. 3: 399–415.
Tapias, Maria, and Xavier Escandell. 2011. "Not in the Eyes of the Beholder: Envy among Bolivian Migrants in Spain." *International Migration* 49, no. 6: 74–94.
Taussig, Michael. 1980. "Reification and the Consciousness of the Patient." *Social Science and Medicine* 14:3–13.
———. 1987. *Shamanism, Colonialism and the Wild Man: A Study in Terror and Healing*. Chicago: University of Chicago Press.
Toranzo Roca, Carlos. 1997. "Informal and Illicit Economies and the Role of Narcotrafficking." In Léons and Sanabria 1997, 195–210.
Tousignant, Michael. 1984. "Pena in the Ecuadorian Sierra: A Psychoanthropological Analysis of Sadness." *Culture, Medicine and Psychiatry* 8:381–98.
Tsing, Ana L. 2005. *Friction: An Ethnography of Global Connection*. Princeton, N.J.: Princeton University Press.
Turner, Terence. 1994. "Bodies and Antibodies: Flesh and Fetish in Contemporary Social Theory." In Csordas 1994, 27–47.
Van Esterick, Penny. 2002. "Contemporary Trends in Infant Feeding Research." *Annual Review of Anthropology* 31:257–78.
Van Schaik, Eileen. 1989. "Paradigms Underlying the Study of Nerves as a Popular Illness Term in Eastern Kentucky." *Medical Anthropology* 11, no. 1: 15–28.
Van Vleet, Krista. 2002. "The Intimacies of Power: Rethinking Violence and Affinity in the Bolivian Andes." *American Ethnologist* 29, no. 3: 567–601.
———. 2003. "Partial Theories: On Gossip, Envy and Ethnography in the Andes." *Enthnography* 4, no. 4: 491–519.
———. 2005. "Dancing on the Borderlands: Girls (Re)Fashioning National Belonging in the Andes." In Canessa 2005b, 107–29.
———. 2008. *Performing Kinship: Narrative, Gender, and the Intimacies of Power in the Andes*. Austin: University of Texas Press.
———. 2009. "'We Had Already Come to Love Her': Raising Children at the Margins of the Bolivian State." *Journal of Latin American and Caribbean Anthropology* 14, no. 1: 1–23.
Velayutham, Selvaraj, and Amanda Wise. 2005. "Moral Economies of a Translocal Village: Obligation and Shame among South Indian Transnational Migrants." *Global Networks* 5, no. 1: 27–47.

Vertovec, Steven. 2004a. "Cheap Calls: The Social Glue of Migrant Transnationalism." *Global Networks* 4, no. 2: 219–24.
———. 2004b. "Migrant Transnationalism and Modes of Transformation." *International Migration Review* 38, no. 3: 970–1001.
Vilas, Carlos M. 2008. "Lynchings and Political Conflict in the Andes." *Latin American Perspectives* 35, no. 162: 103–18.
Walmsley, Emily. 2008. "Raised by Another Mother: Informal Fostering and Kinship Ambiguities in Northwest Ecuador." *Journal of Latin American and Caribbean Anthropology* 13, no. 1: 169–95.
Weismantel, Mary J. 1988. *Food, Gender, and Poverty in the Ecuadorian Andes*. Philadelphia: University of Pennsylvania Press.
———. 1995. "Making Kin: Kinship Theory and Zumbagua Adoptions." *American Ethnologist* 22, no. 4: 685–709.
———. 2001. *Cholas and Pishtacos: Stories of Race and Sex in the Andes*. Chicago: University of Chicago Press.
———. 2005. "Afterword: Andean Identities: Multiplicities, Socialities, Materialities." In Canessa 2005b, 181–94.
White, Luise. 2000. *Speaking with Vampires: Rumor and History in Colonial Africa*. Berkeley: University of California Press.
Whitesell, Lily. 2008. "And Those Who Left: Portraits of a Bolivian Exodus." In *Dignity and Defiance*. Shultz and Draper 2008, 255–90. Berkeley: University of California Press.
Wilkinson, Iain. 2001. "Thinking with Suffering." *Cultural Values* 5, no. 4: 421–44.
———. 2004. "The Problem of 'Social Suffering': The Challenge to Social Science." *Health Sociology Review* 13, no. 2: 113–21.
Wise, Amanda, and Adam Chapman. 2005. "Introduction: Migration, Affect and the Senses." Special issue. *Journal of Intercultural Studies* 26, no. 1: 1–3.
Wolf, Diane L. 2002. "There Is No Place Like 'Home': Emotional Transnationalism and the Struggles of Second Generation Filipinos." In *The Changing Face of Home: The Transnational Lives of the Second Generation*, edited by Peggy Levitt and Mary C. Waters, 255–94. New York: Russell Sage.
Zeitlyn, Sushila, and Rabeya Rowshan. 1997. "Privileged Knowledge and Mothers' 'Perceptions': The Case of Breast-Feeding and Insufficient Milk in Bangladesh." *Medical Anthropology Quarterly* 11, no. 1: 56–68.

Index

Page numbers in italics refer to illustrations.

Abu-Lughod, Lila, 14, 50
aire (in biomedicine, stroke), 10, 11, 46–47
Alejandro (migrant to Spain), 119
ambition: ambivalence about, 83–88, 95–97, 103–4; envy as suppression of, 115–20, 122–23; modernism/progress discourse and, 42; secrecy/nondisclosure and, 120–22; social expectation and, 23. *See also* envy; sorcery
Ana, 11
Andrea, 10
anger: accounts of sickness from, 9, 47; economic distress and, 34, 83; emotional privilege and, 50–54, 97–98, 100–101; as fluid, 45; laughter as relief from, 47; motherhood and, 57; *Pachamama* and, 11, 98; transmission of, 10, 45, 49
anthropology: anthropology of emotion, 12–14, 131; ethnography, 8; fieldwork for this book, 17–20; narratives of emotion and, 13; reflexive anthropology, 16. *See also* medical anthropology
anti-globalization resistance, 4–5, 8, 129–30
Argentina (as migration destination), 1, 3, 11, 23, 33, 69, 71, 105–6
arrebato: defined, 135n6 (Chapter 4); Doña Flora diagnosis, 98; failed sociality and, 10; social power and, 65–66; transmission of, 49, 60, 62–64, 74–75
Augustín, 101

Banzer, Hugo, 32
Barbalet, Jack M., 15
Basso, Keith, 107
Beatty, Andrew, 13
Benita, 88–93
Biehl, João, 12–13
blame: employer responsibility and, 62; jealousy and, 63; maternal responsibility and, 62–63, 66; sorcery and, 37–38
body: bile as channel for emotions, 48; breast milk as channel for emotions, 10, 17, 45, 48–49, 59–62, 65–66, 134n1–2 (Chapter 3); constructivist approach to emotions and, 108–9; embodiment of emotion, 15–16, 45–46, 74–75; emotional elimination through uterus, 48; failures of the body, 11; hydraulic conception of, 45; lived-in body approach, 15; in medical anthropology, 13–14; religious confession of physical ailments, 43–45; social conceptualization of disease and, 9. *See also* embodiment
Bolivia: agrarian reforms of 1953, 30; anti-globalization movement in, 8; anti-neoliberalism protests, 4–5, 129–30; family connections of author, 16–17; GTZ healthcare initiative, 20–21, 29; late-1990s economic reforms, 3–4; map, 5; neoliberal decentralization and policy reforms, 28–30; 1980s "lost decade," 28–29. *See also* Chapare region; Punata; Valle Alto
Bombori, 22, 77

Brazil, 45
breastfeeding, 10, 17, 45, 48–49, 59–63, 65–66, 134n1–2 (Chapter 3)
Buechler, Hans, 79–80
Buechler, Judith-Maria, 79–80
Buechler, Simone, 79–80
Bush, George H. W., 31
Butler, Judith, 35

Canessa, Andrew, 35
capitalization. *See* privatization
Carina, 25–26
Cesar (migrant to Spain), 122–24
Chapare region: economic opportunities in, 58–59, 105; taxi service, 32, 64–66, 134n2 (Chapter 1); war on drugs and, 1, 65–66
Chapman, Adam, 108
chicha: *chicherías* (corn beer halls), 20, 22, 39, 52–53; drinking practices, 127; drinking rituals for, 38–40; envy associated with, 83; *pendón* (*chichería* flagpole), 52; as relief from emotions, 47, 52–53; Tata Bombori pilgrimage and, 91
children: *debilidad* (susceptibility to illness), 67–69, 73–75; emotional disease accounts, 10–11; emotional privilege and, 51; family roles of, 37; market employment of mothers and, 79; maternal transmission of emotions, 45–46, 49–50, 65–68, 74–75. *See also* families; motherhood
class: *debilidad* as social marker, 74; drink preference as class marker, 91; emotional privilege and, 50–54; entrepreneurial social type and, 34–35; *inmobiliarias* and, 73; market clientele and, 51–54; middle class economic distress, 76; out-migration tourist passing, 33–34; social identity, 36
Claudia, 131
coca/cocaine industry: Banzer "coca zero" eradication program, 32; coca leaf traditional usage, 11, 18, 30–31; economic precariousness and, 58–59; *inmobiliarias* and, 70–73; neoliberal reforms and, 30–31; peripheral industries, 64–66; role in national economy, 31–32; unemployment rate and, 4. *See also* war on drugs
Colombia, 31
compadrazgo ritual kinship, 26–27, 38
constructivism, 14, 108–9
Costa, 63
craving (*deseo*/desire), 11, 49–50

Crecensio, Father (parish priest), 27, 42, 82
crying, 47

Das, Veena, 42, 131
debilidad (weakness; susceptibility to illness), 67–69, 73–75
decentralization. *See* privatization
deseo (desire), 11, 49–50
disease: anthropology of emotion and, 12–14; gastrointestinal disease, 1–2, 10; hours of danger for, 54–55; paralysis, 10; perambulation of, 67–68; persistence of emotional illness, 131; religious confession of physical ailments, 43–45; social conceptualization of, 7, 9; social suffering, 3–4; women's economic precariousness and, 57–58. *See also* health; *susto*
domestic violence: accounts of, 10, 59, 65–66, 69, 73; difficulty of marriage and, 37; as everyday violence, 6; workshops/information availability for, 70. *See also* families; gender
Dora (migrant to Spain), 119

economy: Bolivian decentralization policy reforms, 28–30; bribery, 41; coca/cocaine industry and, 31–32; *compadrazgo* ritual kinship contracts, 26–27, 38; economic class disparity, 10; education as social capital, 94–95; *inmobiliarias* (investment/savings instruments), 70–73; measurement of economic growth, 130; motherhood and, 57–58; neoliberalism in state economies, 7; 1980s "lost decade," 28–29; *pasanaku* (rotating credit association), 86; post-privatization overview, 105–7; Spanish labor market and, 109–11; traditional reciprocity, 10, 39–40; triple roles of women, 52; unemployment rate, 29, 41; women's economic precariousness and, 57–61. *See also* informal economy
Ecuador, 45–46, 79–80
Elisa (wife of Juan), 59, 64–66, 74
Elvira, 96–98, 99–101
embodiment: anthropological research on, 15–16; Bombori narratives and, 78; of broader political economic relationships, 2, 129; constructivist approach to, 109; economic reform and, 3–6, 74–75; of failed sociality, 10, 44–45; health effects from distress, 82, 129; of maternal emo-

tions, 74; norms of emotional continence/expression and, 3–6; Punata spirituality and, 46; secrecy/nondisclosure and, 112. *See also* body
embolio (in biomedicine, stroke), 46–47
emigration. *See* migration
Emma (mother of Marta), 88–93
emotions: anthropology of emotion and, 12–14; breastfeeding and, 59–62, 65–66, 134n1–2 (Chapter 3); constructivist approach, 14, 108–9; discharge of, 46, 54; domestic violence and, 65–66; embodiment of emotion, 15–16, 45–46; emotional disease accounts, 10–11; endurance of financial instability, 34; experience of neoliberalism and, 129; failed sociality and, 10; personal narrative and, 11–14; pregnancy emotions, 67–69, 73–75; responses to social and economic factors, 9; transmission to others, 10, 45–46; transnational nondisclosure and, 107–8, 111–16. *See also* anger; *deseo*; envy; maternal emotions; *pena*; preoccupation; *renegona*; *susto*; *tirisya*
envy: ambition in market women and, 87, 91–93; confession as relief from, 44; Doña Flora *envidia* treatment, 98–99, 101–2; economic distress and, 34; link to illness, 9, 15, 42; neoliberal middle class and, 42, 76–78, 82–83; prevention of, 56–57; as private emotion, 116–17; purification ritual for, 89; Spanish labor market and, 118–121; suppression of ambition and, 115–120, 122–23; Tata Bombori and, 78, 91–93; transmission of, 45. *See also* ambition; sorcery
Escandell, Xavier, 135n2 (Chapter 5)
ethnicity: *cholo/chola* designation, 36, 80, 93–94; emotional privilege and, 50–54; out-migration tourist passing, 33–34; social identity and, 36. *See also* identity
Eulalia, 39
Eustaquia, 18

families: construction of relatedness, 45–46; economic distress and, 69–71; as economic safety nets, 6; failed sociality and, 10; honorific kinship, 50–51; male unemployment and, 64–66, 79; maternal transmission of emotions, 45–46, 49–50, 65–68, 74–75; relations with ethnographic

subjects and, 17, 20; remittances from migrants to, 33, 105–7, *106*; separated families, 107; sexual infidelity, 37–38; social identities in, 37. *See also* children; domestic violence; gender
Farmer, Paul, 12
Farthing, Linda, 31
Ferguson, James, 121–22
feria del Martes (Tuesday market), 20–21, 40–41
Fernando (son of Rosalía), 68–69, 73–74
FINSA (*inmobiliria*), 71–73
Flora: advice/help for children, 84, 134n5 (Chapter 4); on breastfeeding, 63; on chicha, 40; consultation with naturalist, 11; on emotional illness, 2, 60; market routine of, 26, 47; Mother's Day celebration, 127–28; Tata Bombori and, 85, 93–104
folk medicine. *See* medicinals; naturalists
food industrial sector, 28
Foucault, Michel, 14–15, 35
fuerza (strength; resistance to disease), 67–68

gender: anthropological research and, 17; chicha consumption and, 40–41, 53; emotional privilege and, 50–54; family roles and, 37; market shopping and, 27; social identity and, 36; Spanish labor market and, 110–11. *See also* domestic violence; families; identity; men; women
Good, Byron, 12–13
gossip, 19–20, 116–17
Graciela, 83
Greenhouse, Carol J., 8
Guillermo (grandson of Flora), 127–28

healers. *See* naturalists; sorcery; *yatiris*
health. *See* disease; *fuerza*; *tranquilas*
herbalists. *See* naturalists
hours of danger, 54–55
humor, 115–16
Hymes, Dell, 107

identity: bribery as civic validation, 41; *cholo/chola* designation, 36, 80, 93–94; *debilidad* as social marker, 74; emotional privilege and, 102; male unemployment and, 64–66, 79; neoliberalism and, 4, 34–35; out-migration tourist passing, 33–34; self-reliance discourse, 9–10, 34, 76, 78; social self, 35–36. *See also* ethnicity; gender

immigration. *See* migration
informal economy: *feria del Martes* role in, 20–21; neoliberal reforms and, 30; unemployment rate and, 4. *See also* economy
inmobiliarias (investment/savings instruments), 70–73
International Monetary Fund (IMF), 3–4, 28
Isabela (wife of Joaquín), 111–12

jealousy. *See* envy
Joaquín (husband of Isabela), 111–12
Joaquin (son of Marta), 86
Juan (husband of Elisa), 59, 64–66
Juan (husband of Flora; father of Mariana), 26, 40, 94–95
Juana, 62
Julio (migrant to Spain), 122–24
Justina, 10–11
Justino (employee of Flora), 26

Kleinman, Arthur, 12–13, 42
Kohl, Benjamin H., 31

Laslett, Barbara, 11
laughter, 47
Laura, 62–63
leche gatona, 60–62
Livingston, Julie, 9
Lucía (migrant to Spain), 112–14
lugares virgenes (virgin places), 55
Lutz, Catherine, 14, 46, 50
Lyon, Margot L., 15

machismo, 37–38
Marcela (daughter of Rosalía), 68–69
Marcela (migrant to Spain), 122–24
Margheritis, Ann, 130
Maria (migrant to Spain), 119
Mariana (daughter of Flora and store owner), 26, 63–64, 84, 94–96, 99, 100, 127–28
Mariano (neighbor of Juan), 65
Marta (mother of Joaquin), 37, 61–62, 85–93, 127–28
maternal emotions: breast milk and, 10, 17, 45, 48–49, 59–62, 65–66, 134n1–2 (Chapter 3); embodiment of, 74; pregnancy emotions, 67–69, 73–75; transmission to children, 45–46, 49–50, 65–68, 74–75. *See also* emotions; motherhood; women
Maynes, Mary Jo, 11

medical anthropology: author training in, 16–17; conceptions of body in, 13–14; on structural violence, 76. *See also* naturalists
medicinals, 17, 25, 66. *See also* naturalists
men: chicha and, 53; emotional privilege and, 51–52; machismo, 37–38, 51; sexual infidelity, 37–38; unemployment and, 64. *See also* gender; women
Mesa, Carlos, 130
migration—international: Cochabamba region emigration tradition, 105–6; envy in migrant communities, 116–24; history of Valle Alto outmigration, 30; migrant-homeland relationships, 123–25; migrant solidarity, 124; remittances and, 33, 105–7, 106; transnational nondisclosure, 107–8, 111–16, 124–25; travel agencies and, 33–34
migration—rural-to-urban, 30
Miguel, 98–99, 102
Miles, Ann, 61
mining industry, 28–29
Monica (migrant to Spain), 122–24
Morales, Evo, 4, 130–31
Moser, Caroline, 52
motherhood: economy and, 57–58; market employment and, 79; maternal responsibility, 62–63, 66; maternal transmission of emotions, 45–46, 49–50, 65–68, 74–75; Mother's Day celebration, 127–28; pregnancy emotions, 67–69, 73–75. *See also* children; women

naturalists (traditional healers): Doña Flora *envidia* treatment, 98–99, 101–2; emotional distress of infants and, 49; extraction/discharge of emotions, 46; fieldwork with, 22; medicinals, 17, 25, 66; Tata Bombori pilgrimage and, 78, 88–89
neoliberalism: defined, 7–8; anti-globalization resistance, 4–5, 8, 129–30; Bolivian decentralization policy reforms, 28–30; effect on middle class, 76; elimination of administrative and educational employment, 80; embodiment of emotion and, 74–75; entrepreneurial social type and, 34–35; globalization and, 7–8; IMF neoliberal reforms, 3–4; *inmobiliarias* and, 70–73; measurement of growth and, 130; middle-class envy and, 76–78; moral/experiential dimensions of, 129; Punata everyday life

and, 27–28; Punateño/a view of the Bolivian state, 41; self-reliance discourse in, 7–8, 9–10, 34, 76, 78, 129
Norma (employee of Wanda), 26

Orr, David, 44
Oths, Katherine, 61

Pachamama: defined, 135n6 (Chapter 4); Doña Flora diagnosis, 98; drinking rituals for, 38–39; failed sociality and, 10; hours/places of danger for, 55; as religious illness, 11
Paola, 32
pasanaku (rotating credit association), 86
Patricia, 130
Paz Estensoro, Victor, 28
pena (sorrow): accounts of, 68; chicha and, 53; crying as relief from, 47; economic distress and, 9–11, 34, 83; emotional privilege and, 50–54; as fluid, 45; link to illness, 15; Pachamama and, 11; Tata Bombori and, 92; transmission of, 10, 45, 49; women's economic precariousness and, 60–61
Pereira, Anthony, 130
Peru, 31, 79–80
Pierce, Jennifer L., 11
pining, 15
places of danger, 55
Portes, Alejandro, 124
Potosí, Bolivia, 46
preoccupation, 49
privatization: Bolivian policy reforms, 29–30; elimination of administrative and educational employment, 80; infrastructural improvements from, 105–6; neoliberalism and, 7–8; privatization of water services, 129–30; self-reliance discourse and, 78; transformation of gender roles and, 79
Punata: accounts of economic decline, 32–33; anti-neoliberalism sentiment in, 4–5; Centro Virgin del Rosario, 21; chicherías (corn beer halls), 20, 22; emotional privilege and, 50–54; feria del Martes (Tuesday market), 20–21; map location, 5; out-migration from, 33–34; overview, 17–18; public services, 26, 133n1 (Chapter 1); Punata hospital, 1–2, 18–21, 27, 70; social identity in, 36; transmission of emotion in, 46; typical domestic decor, 56–57. See also Punata central market; Valle Alto
Punata central market: ambition in market women, 83–88, 95–97; caseras (regular clients), 19, 80, 94, 134n6; clientele social class and, 51–54; market routine of vendors, 26, 47; meat vendors, 26, 32, 68, 80, 81, 84, 93–94; photo, 19; puesto fijo vs. ambulante, 81; resolution of conflicts in, 51; social geography of, 81–82; Tata Bombori importance in, 85–88; as women's social hub, 17–20; women vendors, 42, 52, 78–80

rage. See anger
Rebhun, Linda A., 45
religion: confession of physical ailments, 43–45; evangelicalism, 134n5; motherhood and, 62; Pachamama as religious illness, 11; sorcery and, 43, 82, 121. See also sorcery; Tata Bombori
renegona (volatile), 62
resistance (anti-globalization), 4–5, 8, 129–30
Rita (daughter of Doña Elvira), 99
ritualists. See naturalists
Rosa (mother of Soraya), 114–15
Rosalía (mother of Fernando), 11, 59, 68–74
Rouse, Roger, 108

Sabrina, 56–57
Sánchez de Lozada, Gonzalo, 29, 130
Sandra (newspaper vendor), 27
Santa Cruz, 81, 115, 135n5 (Chapter 5)
saqra horas (hours of danger), 55
Sarita, 32
Scheper-Hughes, Nancy, 6
Seligmann, Linda J., 79–80, 94
Selma, 25
sociality: central market gossip tradition, 19–20; chicha drinking rituals and, 39–40; compadrazgo ritual kinship and, 38; emotional privilege and, 50–54, 97–98, 100–103; failed sociality, 10, 41–42; mistrust over success and, 118–21; transmission of emotions, 10, 45
social meaning of disease, 7, 9. See also disease
social suffering: defined, 3–4; accumulation of emotion/distress and, 47–48; anthropology of emotion and, 12–14; everyday violence and, 6; failed sociality and, 10

Soledad, 25
Sonia, 63
sonqo nanay, 10
Soraya (daughter of Rosa), 114–15
sorcery: avenging of, 43; economic distress and, 76; envy and, 45, 82–83, 116–17, 121; failed sociality and, 44; infidelity and, 37–38; inhibitions of discussions of, 53. *See also* ambition; envy; religion; Tata Bombori
sorrow. *See pena*
Spain (as migration destination): envy in migrant communities, 116–24; fieldwork in, 22–23; fieldwork with transnational families, 135n2 (Chapter 5); migrant-homeland relationships, 123–25; migrant solidarity, 124; migration experiences, 33–34, 84, 103; remittances from migrants to, 18, 105–7, *106*; Spanish labor market, 109–11; transnational nondisclosure, 107–8, 111–16, 124–25
Susana, 84
susto (fright): failed sociality and, 10; overview, 1–2; scholarly literature on, 15–16; transmission of, 49, 60

Tata Bombori: ambition and, 85–88; Doña Flora fiesta, 103; overview, 77–78, *77*; pilgrimage accounts, 85–93, 103–4. *See also* sorcery
Teresa, 1–3, 61–62, 83
Teresa (migrant to Spain), 112, 120–21
textile industry, 28
tin mining, 30
tirisya (pining), 10–11, 34
tranquilas: defined, 6; breastfeeding and, 60–62, 65–66, 134n1–2 (Chapter 3); neoliberal distress and, 129; Tata Bombori and, 78, 85–86; vomiting and, 47–48
transportation industry: capitalization of, 29; importance of, 21; neoliberalism and, 32; war on drugs and, 64

United States: international alternative crop market and, 32; as migration destination, 16–17, 20, 33, 71. *See also* war on drugs

Valle Alto: Chapare taxi/*truffi* service, 32, 64–66, 134n2 (Chapter 1); *feria del Martes* (Tuesday market), 20–21; GTZ healthcare initiative, 21, 29; location, 4–5, *5*; out-migration from, 30. *See also* Bolivia; Punata
Van Vleet, Krista, 36, 46
Vera, 26, 63, 83, 88–93, 127–28
Vertovec, Steven, 109
violence: everyday violence, 6; structural violence, 76. *See also* domestic violence
vomiting, 47–48

Wanda, 26
war on drugs (U.S.): effect on personal safety, 64–66; "favored nation" certification status, 31–32; *inmobiliarias* and, 72; neoliberal reform and, 4; as trigger for traditional illness, 1–3. *See also* coca/cocaine industry
Weismantel, Mary J., 45–46, 79–80
White, Luise, 116–17
Wilkinson, Iain, 3
Wise, Amanda, 108
women: Andean market women, 78–80; breast milk as channel for emotions, 10, 17, 45, 48–49, 59–62, 65–66, 134n1–2 (Chapter 3); chicha and, 53; economic precariousness and, 57–61; emotional privilege and, 51–52, 97–98, 100–103; maternal transmission of emotions, 45–46, 49–50, 65–68, 74–75; miscarriages, 49; motherhood, 57–58; pregnancy emotions, 67–69, 73–75; triple roles of, 52. *See also* domestic violence; gender; men; motherhood
World Bank, 28

yatiris (sorcerers/healers), 82, 121. *See also* naturalists; sorcery

MARIA TAPIAS is an associate professor of anthropology and an associate dean at Grinnell College.

INTERPRETATIONS OF CULTURE IN THE NEW MILLENNIUM
Peruvian Street Lives: Culture, Power, and Economy
 among Market Women of Cuzco   *Linda J. Seligmann*
The Napo Runa of Amazonian Ecuador   *Michael Uzendoski*
Made-from-Bone: Trickster Myths, Music, and History
 from the Amazon   *Jonathan D. Hill*
Ritual Encounters: Otavalan Modern and Mythic Community
 Michelle Wibbelsman
Finding Cholita   *Billie Jean Isbell*
East African Hip Hop: Youth Culture and Globalization
 Mwenda Ntaragwi
Sarajevo: A Bosnian Kaleidoscope   *Fran Markowitz*
Becoming Mapuche: Person and Ritual in Indigenous Chile
 Magnus Course
Kings for Three Days: The Play of Race and Gender in an
 Afro-Ecuadorian Festival   *Jean Muteba Rahier*
Maya Market Women: Power and Tradition in
 San Juan Chamelco, Guatemala   *S. Ashley Kistler*
Victims and Warriors: Violence, History,
 and Memory in Amazonia   *Casey High*
Embodied Protests: Emotions and Women's
 Health in Bolivia   *Maria Tapias*

The University of Illinois Press
is a founding member of the
Association of American University Presses.

Composed in 10.5/13 Adobe Minion Pro
by Lisa Connery
at the University of Illinois Press
Manufactured by Thomson-Shore, Inc.

University of Illinois Press
1325 South Oak Street
Champaign, IL 61820-6903
www.press.uillinois.edu